W9-ACD-314

The Personality Puzzle
Second Edition

INSTRUCTOR'S MANUAL AND TEST-ITEM FILE

The Personality Puzzle

SECOND EDITION

David C. Funder
UNIVERSITY OF CALIFORNIA, RIVERSIDE

WITH EXAM QUESTIONS BY
R. Michael Furr
APPALACHIAN STATE UNIVERSITY

Jana S. Spain
HIGHPOINT UNIVERSITY

David C. Funder
UNIVERSITY OF CALIFORNIA, RIVERSIDE

 W • W • NORTON & COMPANY • NEW YORK • LONDON

ISBN 0-393-97718-8 (pbk.)

W. W. Norton & Company, Inc., 500 Fifth Avenue, New York, NY 10110
   www.wwnorton.com

W. W. Norton & Company Ltd., Castle House, 75/76 Wells Street, London W1T 3QT

1 2 3 4 5 6 7 8 9 0

CONTENTS

PREFACE

Teaching a course in personality psychology is a challenging assignment in several respects. First, although the topic touches on many issues that students find intrinsically interesting, it also includes a mass of historical and technical detail that can, if not handled carefully, hide the forest behind the trees. Second, the field includes historically important megatheories, such as Freud's; philosophical perspectives, such as existentialism; and empirical studies that address technical matters such as factor analyses of personality traits and cognitive processes in goal setting. Tying these together into a coherent package that students find meaningful is no small task.

The Personality Puzzle attempts to accomplish this task. It emphasizes topics students are likely to find interesting; at the same time, it tries to provide a sophisticated and rigorous analysis of these topics. And it covers both historically and philosophically important perspectives, and modern research. But when this book is used as part of a personality course, it is the instructor who brings the content of the course to life. The purpose of this manual is to provide a bit of help.

Plan of the Manual

For each chapter in the text, the manual begins with an outline and summary. Then I provide a few comments on the content of the chapter from an instructor's perspective, offer some suggestions on how to teach this content, and point to the relevance between material in the chapter and the selections in the accompanying reader, *Pieces of the Personality Puzzle*, Second Edition, edited by myself and Daniel J. Ozer. Finally, I list some discussion questions that might be useful in a small class or in sections of a larger class.

This manual also includes questions for course exams. These could be used as is or adapted for a particular instructor's emphasis.

Selling Personality Psychology

Before beginning with the chapter-by-chapter commentary, a few general remarks are in order. First, as emphasized in the Preface to the text, the principal aim of the personality course as I teach it is to persuade students that personality psychology matters. All too often we hear psychologists lament that the general public neither understands nor appreciates our field. The person on the street identifies psychology with clinical psychology and often sees it as so much witch doctoring. The public does not understand that psychology is a field of science that gathers and analyzes data and tries to account for those data with rigorously developed theories.

But if that description of the public is true, who is at fault? Given the number of people who now go to college and the large percentage of those who take psychology courses, the only ones psychologists should blame for any public misunderstanding of their field is themselves. This is our big chance. If we bore our students, bog them down in trivia, or talk over their heads, we should not be surprised if they decide our field is a waste of time and money. But if we can engage them, show them what psychology can teach them about their lives, and excite them about the same issues that we find exciting, the results will be good for both the students and psychology.

This is what I mean when I say that the purpose of *The Personality Puzzle* is to sell psychology. It does not mean I wish to neglect an education in research methods, theoretical content, or empirical research. But if, at the end of the course, the student does not understand why any of these are important, then it is not clear what he or she has really learned.

My first piece of advice, therefore, is to touch on the real-life concerns of your students with the material of this course whenever you can. The purpose is not to turn personality into a field of pop psychology or to "dumb down" the course. Rather, it is to act on the knowledge that if college professors do not explain to their students why psychology is important, it is unlikely anybody else ever will.

Changes from the First Edition

The philosophy, style, and even much of the content of the First Edition remain unchanged. However, several changes are important to note for an instructor who has used the First Edition.

First and most obviously, the chapter organization has been changed in a small but important way. The coverage of the psychoanalytic approach has been reorganized from four chapters to three. This change represents only a slight deemphasis of the approach. Most of the First Edition content is still here, and I have added a good deal of recent research on psychoanalytic topics, including empirical investigations of defense mechanisms. At the same time, the cognitive approach to personality has been moved out of the behaviorist and social learning section and promoted to a section of its own, with two chapters. These chapters include an updated description of the general cognitive system that contrasts the traditional serial model with more recent parallel models. They also include an updated treatment of Mischel's CAPS model and an all-new summary of Epstein's cognitive-experiential self system.

A second noticeable change is that the basic types of data considered in Chapter 2 have been renamed and reorganized. They are now called B, L, I, and S data. The "T-data" label for direct behavioral observation continued to confuse students and so now this type is called B data. The presentation begins with S (self-report) data because that seems like the most obvious source of information for finding out about a person, then moves (in order) through I, L, and B data.

Third, least obviously, but most pervasively, the book has been updated in numerous large and small ways throughout. Personality psychology is a busy field and its activity seems to be accelerating. Frankly, I was surprised to find so much new material to include. New material is particularly abundant in the biological, cognitive and psychoanalytic sections, but every chapter has something new in it. As a result, the Second Edition is about one hundred pages longer than the first.

Other Matters

Two final comments. First, even though it has grown since the First Edition, the coverage of the text remains selective. Obviously, *The Personality Puzzle* is not one of those twelve-pound tomes that attempt to be encyclopedic in their coverage. I hope this fact has two advantages. First, the book might be a bit more readable than some of its hefty cousins. Second, its selectivity opens many areas for instructor-developed lectures that will not overlap the book. For example, an instructor with a particular interest and expertise in the neo-Freudians or the modern cognitive approaches will find both represented in the book but with much more left that he or she may choose to offer to the students. I will point out other possibilities in the sections that follow.

Finally, this is an opinionated text. I did not take the plain-vanilla approach to textbook writing; this means that there is room for disagreement in many places. I would urge an instructor who thinks me wrong on a particular point to explain to his or her students just how and why. I would further urge such an instructor to be careful in how such disagreements are handled. I have found—the hard way—that if I tell students that some other psychologist disagrees with me because that psychologist is ignorant or confused, students conclude that *everybody* in psychology is ignorant and confused. Although we psychologists are somewhat notorious for getting carried away in the heat of our disagreements with one another, the more objectively, analytically, and respectfully we can explain such disagreements to our students, the more likely they are to find the topics worth their own serious thought.

CHAPTER 1 | The Study of the Person

OUTLINE

I. The Goal of Personality Psychology
   A. Mission Impossible
   B. Competitors or Complements?
   C. Distinct Approaches versus the OBT
   D. On Advantages as Disadvantages and Vice Versa
II. The Plan of this Book
III. Pigeonholing versus Appreciation of Individual Differences
IV. Summary

SUMMARY

Personality psychology's unique mission is to try to explain the psychological functioning of whole individuals. This is an impossible mission, however, so different approaches to personality must limit themselves in various ways. Personality psychology can be organized into six basic approaches: trait, biological, psychoanalytic, phenomenological, behavioral, and cognitive. Each addresses certain aspects of human psychology quite well and ignores others. The advantages and disadvantages of each approach seem inseparable. The book is grouped into six sections that survey each basic approach. Sometimes regarded as a demeaning attempt to pigeonhole people, personality psychology's real implication is an appreciation of the ways in which each individual is unique.

ABOUT THE CHAPTER

As introductory chapters go, this one is fairly brief. It introduces and defines personality, briefly, and explains that the topic is so broad it must be divided into

1

five basic approaches. In a change from the First Edition, the cognitive approach is now separated out from the behavioral and social learning approaches.

An important point emphasized throughout the book, and perhaps worth mentioning in lecture, is that the basic approaches are not different answers to the same question, they are different questions. Another way to say this is that the different sections of the book are not really about different, competing accounts of the same phenomena. To a large extent, the different sections are about different topics.

It also might be worth mentioning the truism in science—which will be new to most students—that in research the questions are more important than the answers. Answers always change over time; certain questions are eternal. The basic questions asked by the six basic approaches to personality may be among these.

The most unusual aspect of this chapter is probably its promise that personality psychology is interesting and that the book will not bore them. This promise will not be fulfilled for all students, but I hope it works for many. If nothing else, I hope students find it refreshing to see a text promise to try to be interesting, rather than take the attitude that "this is difficult material and if you find it boring, that's too bad." Please note that the chapter does not promise the material will be simple. Simple material is not often interesting, and the book that follows is not simple.

TEACHING NOTES

One exercise I often do at the beginning of the course, before anything else, is to ask students this: If you could ask an expert who knew everything about human psychology one question, what would that question be? I have them write their responses, hand them in, and then I read a subset of them aloud (either right then or at the next class meeting). It is interesting to note that easily 70 to 80 percent of the questions students ask fall within the domain of personality psychology. This is a good way to make the points (1) personality is at the center of what people ordinarily mean by the term *psychology*, and (2) a course and book that cover questions like these ought to be interesting and valuable.

Then it is time to begin presenting course material. In my own course, I seem to present less introductory material every year. I found that few of the abstract, overview-type comments that I used to make meant anything to my students. In particular, I found that the first (or second) day of the term is not a good time to compare and contrast alternative paradigms, comment on the place of personality psychology within the field as a whole, or editorialize about my favorite approach. Instead, I try to motivate their interest in the topic (as described above), and *briefly* outline and define the basic approaches to be covered. I also tell them, for the first of what will be many times, that the different approaches are better characterized by the different questions they ask than by the competing answers they offer.

PIECES OF THE PERSONALITY PUZZLE

From Part I, the piece by Dan McAdams, "What Do We Know When We Know a Person?" raises all the right issues for the beginning of a personality course. Of course, the best question he raises is the one in his title, which is another excellent topic for course discussion. One could have this discussion, based on the same question, on both the first *and* last day of the course. It would be fascinating to take notes on the first day and then compare what is said to the answers offered on the last day.

DISCUSSION QUESTIONS

1. What do we know when we know a person?

2. What is the purpose of psychology? What kinds of questions should a science of psychology seek to answer?

3. Why are you taking this course? What do you hope to learn? What use do you expect it to be?

4. If you could choose what this course was to be about, what would you ask for? Why?

5. Which is more important, answers or questions? (This discussion could lead into some elementary philosophy of science with which an instructor so inclined could prepare students for material to come later in the course.)

MULTIPLE-CHOICE QUESTIONS

1. Personality is an individual's characteristic patterns of
   a. behavior.
   b. emotion.
   c. thought.
   d. all of the above.

   Answer: d   Page: 2
   Topic: The Goal of Personality Psychology

2. The unique mandate of personality psychologists is to attempt to
   a. identify and measure individual differences in ability and behavior.
   b. determine the effect of the social environment on behavior.
   c. explain whole, functioning persons in their social context.
   d. prevent or treat psychological personality disorders.

   Answer: c   Page: 2
   Topic: The Goal of Personality Psychology

3. Personality psychologists who adhere to the _____ focus on identifying, conceptualizing, and measuring the ways that people differ psychologically from one another.
   a. psychoanalytic approach
   b. trait approach
   c. cognitive approach
   d. phenomenological approach

   Answer: b   Page: 3
   Topic: Mission Impossible

4. Personality psychologists adhering to the _____ focus on psychic energy, the workings of the unconscious mind, and the nature and resolution of internal mental conflict.
   a. psychoanalytic approach
   b. trait approach
   c. cognitive approach
   d. phenomenological approach

   Answer: a   Page: 3
   Topic: Mission Impossible

5. Psychologists following the phenomenological approach
   a. focus primarily on the workings of the unconscious mind and the resolution of internal mental conflict.
   b. study how our overt behavior is affected by rewards and punishments.
   c. build theoretical models of how people process information.
   d. are concerned with our conscious experience of the world and the consequences of having free will.

   Answer: d   Page: 3
   Topic: Mission Impossible

6. The personality paradigm that focuses on rewards and punishments is the
   a. trait paradigm.
   b. behaviorist paradigm.
   c. phenomenological paradigm.
   d. psychoanalytic paradigm.

   Answer: b   Page: 3
   Topic: Mission Impossible

7. _____ theories focus on how the basic processes of perception, memory, and thought affect behavior and personality.
   a. Psychoanalytic
   b. Trait

c. Cognitive
d. Phenomenological

Answer: c   Page: 3
Topic: Mission Impossible

8. The task of an employer who compares many job applicants in an attempt to identify one dependable, conscientious, and hard-working individual to hire is similar to that of the _____ psychologist who attempts to identify and assess individual differences.
   a. psychoanalytic
   b. trait
   c. cognitive
   d. behavioral

Answer: b   Page: 4
Topic: Mission Impossible

9. Jeff suspects that his roommate's sexist jokes may indicate he has some hidden, unconscious hostility toward women or that he feels very insecure around women. Jeff's analysis suggests a _____ approach to personality.
   a. psychoanalytic
   b. trait
   c. phenomenological
   d. behaviorist

Answer: a   Page: 4
Topic: Mission Impossible

10. Each of the several approaches to personality is good at handling its own key concern
    a. but generally ignores the key concerns of the other approaches.
    b. as well as the key concerns of the other approaches.
    c. and also explains the role of unconscious motivation.
    d. and is very effective at changing behavior.

Answer: a   Page: 4
Topic: Mission Impossible

11. Personality psychology shares with clinical psychology
    a. an emphasis on mental health and the treatment of psychological problems.
    b. a common obligation to try to understand the whole person.
    c. a requirement that both personality psychologists and clinical psychologists be licensed.

d. the fact that both personality psychologists and clinical psychologists are usually in private practice rather than universities.

Answer: b   Page: 2
Topic: The Goal of Personality Psychology

12. What, according to the textbook author, is impossible?
   a. To understand everything about a person all at once
   b. To choose to limit what you look at in a person
   c. To find patterns across different kinds of observation
   d. To make any real progress towards solving the personality puzzle

Answer: a   Page: 2
Topic: Mission Impossible

13. The purpose of a basic approach (or paradigm) is to
   a. expand the range of data you consider.
   b. integrate diverse perspectives.
   c. limit yourself to certain kinds of observations and patterns.
   d. resolve contradictions in data.

Answer: c   Page: 3
Topic: Mission Impossible

14. Advocates of any particular basic approach to personality usually
   a. claim that their approach explains everything worth explaining.
   b. admit that other approaches have their good points.
   c. proudly assert that they have deliberately limited what they have chosen to look at.
   d. claim that approaches cannot be compared to each other.

Answer: a   Page: 4
Topic: Mission Impossible

15. A major theme of your textbook will be
   a. the personality puzzle will never be solved.
   b. One Big Theory (OBT) can account for everything in personality.
   c. great strengths are usually great weaknesses.
   d. a single basic approach must be chosen as best, on the basis of rigorous data analysis.

Answer: c   Page: 6
Topic: Mission Impossible

16. Personality psychology emphasizes how
    a. all people are basically the same.
    b. predicting behavior is impossible.
    c. people are different from each other.
    d. different adults are from children.

    Answer: c   Page: 9
    Topic: Mission Impossible

17. The trait approach, the behaviorist approach, and the psychoanalytic approach
    a. are irreconcilable and contradictory views of human psychology.
    b. are all part of the One Big Theory (OBT).
    c. address the biological basis of human psychology.
    d. address different sets of questions about human psychology.

    Answer: d   Page: 4
    Topic: Mission Impossible

18. Which one of the following statements is false?
    a. Personality psychology is where the rest of psychology comes together.
    b. Personality psychology addresses questions that are entirely separate from the rest of psychology.
    c. Personality psychology draws heavily from social, cognitive, developmental, and biological psychology.
    d. Personality psychology is allied closely with clinical psychology.

    Answer: b   Page: 2
    Topic: Mission Impossible

19. Personality psychology emphasizes how people are _____, and the experimental fields of psychology (like cognitive and social psychology) emphasize how people are _____.
    a. similar to each other; different from each other
    b. different from each other; similar to each other
    c. essentially good; essentially bad
    d. motivated by unconscious forces; motivated by conscious forces

    Answer: b   Page: 9
    Topic: Pigeonholing versus Appreciation of Individual Differences

CHAPTER 2

Clues to Personality:
The Basic Sources of Data

OUTLINE

I. Data Are Clues

II. Four Kinds of Clues

   A. Ask the Person Directly: S data

      1. Advantage: Best expert

      2. Advantage: Causal force

      3. Advantage: Simple and easy

      4. Disadvantage: Maybe they won't tell you

      5. Disadvantage: Maybe they can't tell you

      6. Disadvantage: Too simple and easy

   B. Ask Somebody Who Knows: I data

      1. Advantage: Large amount of information

      2. Advantage: Real-world basis

      3. Advantage: Common sense

      4. Advantage: Causal force

      5. Disadvantage: Limited amount of information

      6. Disadvantage: Error

      7. Disadvantage: Bias

   C. See How the Person Is Faring in Life: L data

      1. Advantage: Intrinsic importance

      2. Advantage: Psychological relevance

      3. Disadvantage: Multidetermination

   D. Watch What the Person Does: B data

      1. Natural B data

      2. Contrived B data

      3. Advantage: Range of contexts

      4. Advantage: Objective and quantifiable

      5. Disadvantage: Uncertain interpretation

      6. Mixed types

III. Conclusion
IV. Summary

SUMMARY

All science begins with observation. The observations a scientist makes are called data. For the scientific study of personality, four kinds of data are available. Each kind has advantages and disadvantages. The S data comprise the person's own self-judgments of his or her own personality. The advantages of S data are that each individual is the best expert about herself or himself, that S data also have a causal force all their own, and that S data are simple and easy to gather. The disadvantages are that people sometimes will not or cannot tell you about themselves and that S data may be so easy to obtain that psychologists use them too much. The I data comprise the judgments of knowledgeable informants about the personality traits of the person being studied. The advantages of I data include that informants' judgments are typically based on large amounts of information, that this information comes from real life, that informants can use common sense, and that the judgments of people who know the person are important because they have a causal force all their own. The disadvantages of I data are that no informant knows everything about another person, that informants' judgments can be biased or participant to errors such as forgetting, and that a few informants may not have common sense.

The L data comprise observable life outcomes such as being arrested, getting sick, or graduating from college. The L data have the advantage of being intrinsically important and of being psychologically relevant at least sometimes, but have the disadvantage of not always being psychologically relevant. The B data comprise direct observations of a person doing something in a testing situation. This situation may be a personality test such as the Rorschach ink blot, a social setting constructed in a psychological laboratory, or the person's real-life environment. The advantages of B data are that they can look at many different kinds of behaviors, including those which might not occur in normal life, and that because B data are obtained through direct observation, they are in a sense objective. The disadvantage of B data is that for all their superficial objectivity, it is still not always clear what they mean psychologically. Because each kind of data for personality research is potentially valuable *and* potentially misleading, researchers should gather and compare all of them.

ABOUT THE CHAPTER

This chapter is about observations. I present a four-part scheme of S, I, L, and B data. Three things are important to note about this scheme. First, this is a change from the First Edition, where B data were called T data and the types were presented in a different order. I have found the T-data label impossible to explain (it stood for "test data") whereas B data (standing for "behavioral data") is fairly self-explanatory.

Second, the present four-part scheme is an adaptation of others with which the instructor might be familiar, such as those by Jack Block and Raymond Cattell. It is not equivalent to those, however. My handling of I and B data, in particular, are different.

Third, many kinds of observations one can imagine fall through the cracks of this (and any other) organizational scheme. I don't think this is a fatal flaw; on the contrary, I think it is a worthwhile exercise to put some effort into coming up with ambiguous cases and deciding where they best fit or what they fit between. It helps students to see the range of data that could be relevant for the study of personality.

I have found that the most difficult material in this chapter to explain is my division of personality tests into those which produce S data and those which produce B data. Indeed, some of my colleagues disagree that this is a useful distinction; an instructor who feels this way should feel free to explain why in lecture. I persist in thinking there is an important difference between direct self-reports (S data) and self-descriptions treated as behavioral samples (B data). By this definition, the Self-monitoring Scale and Stanford Shyness Survey produce S data; the MMPI and the Rorschach test produce B data.

Another unusual aspect of this presentation is that I describe nearly all experiments as gathering B data. That is, they all directly measure some narrow and concrete aspect of a subject's behavior. This categorization means that almost all data gathered by the other subfields of psychology are B data; only personality includes the other three types. It also means that—contrary to claims the students may have heard elsewhere—there is nothing intrinsically superior about direct behavioral observation over other kinds of data because, as the chapter explains, one is never sure about the psychological meaning of B data.

TEACHING NOTES

Research methods is a topic that students will perceive right away as forbidding. It is probably not possible to overcome all of their misgivings, but it is worth a try. One possibility is to point out that the question of methods is simply the question, what do you do to find out something else nobody else knows? If you can't look the answer up in a book, what do you do? The answer is observe the phenomenon, and try to be systematic and organized in how you make your observations, record them, and analyze them. This explanation does not usually make students think methodology is fun, but at least takes it out of the realm of the completely mysterious.

The distinctions between B, L, I, and S data are probably best taught through examples. An instructor could describe some of his or her favorite research studies and ask students which kinds of data are represented. Or, an instructor could ask students to imagine kinds of observations one might make of people, then fit them into the BLIS scheme. Some will be ambiguous, and it is probably not a good idea too be overly dogmatic about which classification is right. The purpose of the BLIS scheme is not to infallibly find an unambiguous slot for all possible data but to illustrate the range of possible data for personality psychology and provide a vocabulary for how one kind of data is different from another.

PIECES OF THE PERSONALITY PUZZLE

The two relevant selections for this chapter are the articles in Part I by Block and by Gosling et al. The Block article is a specific pitch for longitudinal research, which is a topic not emphasized in the text but perhaps worth some mention in lecture. The Block article also mentions the wide range of data his longitudinal project gathers, in terms of his LOST scheme which is similar but not exactly equivalent to the scheme I use. The Gosling article compares two kinds of data, roughly parallel to S and B data.

DISCUSSION QUESTIONS

1. If you wanted to know all about the personality of the person sitting next to you, what would you do?

2. Is there anything about a person that, in your opinion, is impossible to know? Is there anything that is unethical to know?

3. Can you think of kinds of observations—data—that you could make of a person that would fall outside of the BLIS scheme? Which of the four categories comes closest?

4. An experimenter gives a subject a long list of impossible-to-solve mathematics problems. The experimenter times how long the subject works on the problems before throwing them on the floor and giving up in disgust. The minutes-and-seconds measure the experimenter has taken is what kind of data? (B data.) The experimenter calls this measure "a real, behavioral measure of persistence." What is right and wrong about this label?

MULTIPLE-CHOICE QUESTIONS

1. There are no perfect _____ of personality, only _____.
   a. measures; devices
   b. indicators; clues

c. theories; hypotheses
d. reliable measures; valid measures

Answer: b   Page: 13
Topic: Clues to Personality

2. When gathering data or clues about personality, the best policy is to
   a. gather only a very small number of clues and focus attention on the important ones.
   b. gather only those clues which are certain not to be misleading.
   c. rely solely on self-report data.
   d. collect as many clues as possible.

Answer: d   Page: 14
Topic: Data Are Clues

3. Easily observable, real-life outcomes of possible psychological significance are
   a. S data.
   b. B data.
   c. I data.
   d. L data.

Answer: d   Page: 27
Topic: Four Kinds of Clues—L Data

4. Which of the following is an example of L data?
   a. A description of Terry's personality provided by her mother
   b. An observer's count of the number of times Terry laughs during a videotaped laboratory interaction
   c. The number of times Terry has been hospitalized
   d. Terry's response of "true" to the questionnaire item "I enjoy interacting with other people"

Answer: c   Page: 27
Topic: Four Kinds of Clues—L Data

5. The main disadvantage of using L data is
   a. that they may be affected by too many things to tell us much about a person.
   b. that they are descriptions based on hundreds of behaviors in many situations.
   c. that informants may be biased about the person they are judging.
   d. all of the above.

Answer: a   Page: 29
Topic: Four Kinds of Clues—L Data

6. A major disadvantage of L data is
    a. that they provide a large amount of information.
    b. that informants may only have access to a narrow range of the target's behavior.
    c. their multidetermination.
    d. that judges may be biased about the person they are describing.

    Answer: c   Page: 29
    Topic: Four Kinds of Clues—L Data

7. The I data are
    a. self-judgments.
    b. judgments made by knowledgeable observers.
    c. easily observable, real-life outcomes.
    d. direct observations of the subject in some predefined context.

    Answer: b   Page: 20
    Topic: Four Kinds of Clues—I Data

8. Which of the following is *not* an advantage of I data?
    a. They have causal force.
    b. They include common sense.
    c. They are based on large amounts of information.
    d. They come from carefully controlled experimental situations.

    Answer: d   Pages: 21–22
    Topic: Four Kinds of Clues—I Data

9. A personality description of a client by his or her therapist is an example of
    a. S data.
    b. L data.
    c. I data.
    d. B data.

    Answer: c   Page: 20
    Topic: Four Kinds of Clues—I Data

10. The husband of a participant in a personality research study serves as an informant and provides researchers with a description of the participant's personality. The accuracy of his description is suspect because
    a. it may be biased by his relationship with the participant.
    b. it is based on very brief observations of the participant's behavior in only a few situations.

c. informants' judgments generally do not include common sense.

d. all of the above.

Answer: a   Page: 26
Topic: Four Kinds of Clues—I Data

11. Different informants may not agree about the personality of a common target individual because

a. each judge may only see the target person in a limited number of social contexts.

b. judges may form a mistaken impression based on the recollection of a single, uncharacteristic behavior.

c. some informants may have biases that affect the accuracy of their judgments.

d. all of the above.

Answer: d   Pages: 23–27
Topic: Four Kinds of Clues—I Data

12. The judgments of your personality that others form affect your opportunities and expectancies and, as a result, are said to have

a. generalizability.

b. validity.

c. causal force.

d. reliability.

Answer: c   Pages: 22–23
Topic: Four Kinds of Clues—I Data

13. In layperson's terms, I data essentially reflect

a. your internal states or emotions.

b. your level of self-awareness.

c. your reputation.

d. industry data collected in the workplace.

Answer: c   Page: 22
Topic: Four Kinds of Clues—I Data

14. Because Jesse's teacher believes that he is intelligent, she challenges him with extra assignments and generally encourages his curiosity. At the end of the school year, Jesse performs better on the school's achievement test than any of the other students. Jesse's enhanced performance was likely due to the

a. recency effect.

b. expectancy effect.

c. self-serving bias.
d. judgment bias.

Answer: b   Page: 23
Topic: Four Kinds of Clues—I Data

15. The tendency for us to become what other people believe us to be is called the
a. recency effect.
b. expectancy effect.
c. self-serving bias.
d. judgment bias.

Answer: b   Page: 23
Topic: Four Kinds of Clues—I Data

16. While completing the NEO Personality Inventory, you answer "true" to the item "I consider myself a nervous person." Your response to this item would be an example of
a. L data.
b. I data.
c. S data.
d. B data.

Answer: c   Page: 15
Topic: Four Kinds of Clues—S Data

17. The principle behind S data is that
a. only a trained personality psychologist can interpret S data.
b. the best information about personality is obtainable from real-life social outcomes.
c. to assess personality, you must observe what the person actually does.
d. you are the world's best expert about your own personality.

Answer: d   Page: 17
Topic: Four Kinds of Clues—S Data

18. In order to examine the relationship between early life experiences and adult criminality, Dr. Robbins asks his research participants to fill out questionnaires describing their early life. He then obtains access to copies of their arrest records from the county courthouse. The questionnaires used in Dr. Robbins' study would be _____ while the arrest records would be _____.
a. L data; B data
b. S data; I data

c. S data; L data

d. B data; L data

Answer: c   Pages: 15, 27
Topic: Four Kinds of Clues

19. The _____ are the most frequently used basis for personality assessment.

a. B data

b. L data

c. S data

d. I data

Answer: c   Page: 16
Topic: Four Kinds of Clues—S Data

20. Which type of data would most likely yield the best (i.e., most accurate) information about the content of dreams?

a. S data

b. B data

c. L data

d. I data

Answer: a   Page: 17
Topic: Four Kinds of Clues—S Data

21. Dr. Garcia is attempting to determine what emotions people are experiencing when they are fantasizing or daydreaming. To obtain the most accurate information, Dr. Garcia should use

a. L data.

b. I data.

c. S data.

d. B data.

Answer: c   Page: 17
Topic: Four Kinds of Clues—S Data

22. To obtain S data, a psychologist must

a. look up information in public records.

b. recruit informants.

c. observe the subject directly.

d. write up a questionnaire.

Answer: d   Page: 18
Topic: Four Kinds of Clues—S Data

23. The _____ are the most cost-effective data.
    a. S data
    b. L data
    c. I data
    d. B data

    Answer: a   Page: 17
    Topic: Four Kinds of Clues—S Data

24. Data that derive from the researcher's direct observation of what the subject does in some predefined context are
    a. L data.
    b. I data.
    c. S data.
    d. B data.

    Answer: d   Page: 30
    Topic: Four Kinds of Clues—B data

25. Beeper and diary reports can be considered
    a. L data.
    b. I data.
    c. S data.
    d. B data.

    Answer: d   Pages: 30–31
    Topic: Four Kinds of Clues—B data

26. Which of the following would be an example of natural B data?
    a. Reports of the number of times a subject told a joke in a day
    b. The number of seconds a subject waits before seeking help during an experimental emergency situation
    c. A subject's verbal responses to a Rorschach test
    d. The number of times a subject interrupts others during a videotaped laboratory situation

    Answer: a   Page: 30
    Topic: Four Kinds of Clues—B data

27. Asking your coworkers how many times you have stolen a pencil or pen from your employer elicits
    a. L data.
    b. S data.

    c. I data.

    d. B data.

Answer: d   Page: 31

Topic: Four Kinds of Clues—B data

28. The Thematic Apperception Test and the Rorschach test elicit

    a. L data.

    b. I data.

    c. S data.

    d. B data.

Answer: d   Page: 33

Topic: Four Kinds of Clues—B data

29. If, on a personality test, a psychologist asks you a question because he or she wants to know the answer, the test elicits _____. If on a personality test, a psychologist asks you a question because he or she wants to see how you will respond to that stimulus, the test elicits

    _____.

    a. causal force; phenomenological force

    b. S data; I data

    c. S data; B data

    d. contrived B data; natural B data

Answer: c   Page: 33

Topic: Four Kinds of Clues—B data

30. We need to collect clues about personality because

    a. personality is revealed through perfect indicators of thoughts, emotions, and behaviors.

    b. personality tests are unethical.

    c. personality is something that resides, hidden, inside an individual.

    d. S data are not always available.

Answer: c   Page: 13

Topic: Data Are Clues

31. Since each kind of data has limitations, personality psychologists should

    a. not bother collecting data.

    b. gather as much data as possible.

    c. only use L data, which are the most reliable.

    d. only use data that have no limitations.

Answer: b   Page: 14

Topic: Data Are Clues

32. If Dr. O'Connell wants to learn about Laura, why might Dr. O'Connell want to use S data?
    a. The S data have causal force.
    b. The S data are relatively simple and easy to collect.
    c. The person supplying the S data may be the world's best expert about Laura.
    d. All of the above.

    Answer: d   Page: 17
    Topic: Four Kinds of Clues—S Data

33. If Dr. O'Connell wants to learn about Laura, why might Dr. O'Connell want to avoid using S data?
    a. The person supplying the S data may not want or be able to provide accurate reports about Laura.
    b. The S data often do not have psychological relevance.
    c. The S data are influenced by too many societal factors to reveal much about a person's personality.
    d. All of the above.

    Answer: a   Page: 18
    Topic: Four Kinds of Clues—S Data

34. What you do may be influenced by how you see yourself and how you are seen by others. This means that your self-perceptions and others' perceptions have
    a. L-data advantages.
    b. B-data disadvantages.
    c. phenomenological force.
    d. causal force.

    Answer: d   Page: 17
    Topic: Four Kinds of Clues—B data

35. The most important advantage of B data is that they are based on
    a. common sense, so have greater psychological relevance.
    b. a report by the best expert, so are more accurate.
    c. direct biological tests, so have greater causal force and scientific value.
    d. direct observations of behavior, so are more objective and quantifiable.

    Answer: d   Page: 34
    Topic: Four Kinds of Clues—B data

| CHAPTER 3 | Personality Psychology as Science: Research Methods |

OUTLINE

20

SUMMARY

Psychology puts a great deal of emphasis on the methods by which knowledge can be obtained and in general is more concerned with improving our understanding of human nature than with practical applications. Personality psychology particularly emphasizes the reliability, validity, and generalizability of the measurements that it gathers. Reliability refers to the stability or repeatability of measurements. Validity refers to the degree to which a measurement actually measures what it is trying to measure. Generalizability is a broader concept that subsumes both reliability and validity and refers to the class of other measurements to which a given measurement is related. Representative design is a technique used to maximize the generalizability of one's research results. Psychological data are gathered through experimental and correlational designs. Experimental designs manipulate the variable of interest, whereas correlational designs measure a variable as it already exists in the participants being studied. Both approaches have advantages and disadvantages, but the experimental method is the only one that can determine the direction of causality. The best way to summarize research results is in terms of effect size, which describes numerically the degree to which one variable is related to another. One good measure of effect size is the correlation coefficient, which can be evaluated with the Binomial Effect Size Display. Ethical issues relevant to psychology include the way research results are used, truthfulness in science, and the use of deception in research with human participants.

ABOUT THE CHAPTER

This chapter covers a lot of ground. Its treatment of reliability, validity, and generalizability is fairly conventional. Not all texts introduce generalizability, but I find it useful to do so because that leads naturally to a discussion of facets of generalizability including subjects, stimuli, and responses. The Brunswikian notion of representative design is introduced. I believe that to this day Brunswik's fundamental methodological insights are underappreciated and underutilized in psychology.

My treatment of representative design is just one of several aspects of the presentation that could be considered controversial. For example, I compare and contrast correlational and experimental designs. This section of the chapter has been rewritten for the Second Edition, in an attempt to make it clearer. Rather than reach the conventional conclusion—which some students will already have been taught—that experimental designs are intrinsically superior, I note that both designs have advantages and disadvantages.

Although I explain what it is, I take a stand against significance testing. The statistical literature seems to be evolving rapidly toward a widespread recognition of the point that Paul Meehl made many years ago: Significance levels tell you little, if anything, and are often misleading. This message will probably not align with what students have been taught in their statistics classes. An instructor could handle this by noting that the topic is one of current debate and not yet finally resolved, or the instructor could take a stand and either support or argue with my position.

Instead of significance testing, I argue the importance of effect size. The correlation coefficient—my favorite measure of effect size—is briefly explained. I then argue that squaring correlations to yield variance explained is an inappropriate practice. As this practice is one that most students are still taught in introductory statistics classes, this surprising message should probably be handled the same way as the one concerning significance testing: State it is a matter of current controversy (it is), agree, or disagree.

The book takes a fair amount of space explaining the use of Rosenthal and Rubin's Binomial Effect Size Display (BESD). A surprising number of psychologists don't know about this. While visiting a prominent university to present a colloquium, I once drew a blank 2 by 2 table (like Table 3.1 in the text) on the board, added the marginal frequencies, and asked the assembled faculty to guess what number went in the upper left-hand corner for a correlation of .30. The first answer, from a methodological expert, was "52?" (The answer is 65). This kind of distorted estimation is what comes of squaring correlation coefficients and underappreciating their size!

It is hard to read much personality research and not see correlation coefficients everywhere. It is important to understand correctly what kinds of effects are being described. That is why I teach the BESD in my course and in the text.

The chapter concludes with a discussion of ethics. The controversial position I take here is quite a hard line against deception in psychological research. I know this a minority position among psychologists, and I urge instructors who disagree with me (as well as those who agree) to present the argument to their students. The main thing is to get students to think about this issue; it matters less what they conclude than how well their conclusion is reasoned.

TEACHING NOTES

I have already mentioned the several controversial positions taken in this chapter and the ways an instructor might want to handle them.

A classroom demonstration of aggregation, akin to the one with meter sticks described in the text, might be useful.

Finally, I suggest the instructor take a class session and talk about correlation coefficients, how they are calculated, and what they mean. This is such a fundamental number for personality research that it is hard to read much literature at all without understanding what it means. Yet, in my experience, most students come out of their statistics classes with only the fuzziest notion of what a correlation is. Typically so much emphasis was put into computational techniques that little conceptual explanation was proffered. Here is an opportunity to remedy that.

PIECES OF THE PERSONALITY PUZZLE

Several selections in Part II of the reader tie directly to material in this chapter. The reader includes one of Rosenthal and Rubin's original expositions of the BESD, with a clearly presented example of how to do the computation.

Cronbach and Meehl's exposition of construct validity, referred to in the text, is included in the reader. The other classic article in the methodology of personality is the Campbell-Fiske article, also included. I do not discuss the multitrait multimethod matrix in the text, but this topic and the issues of discriminant and convergent validation might be useful to cover in lecture.

The reader also includes a classic article by Harrison Gough concerning the evaluation of validity. Gough's approach is quite different from Cronbach and Meehl's. Among other interesting points, Gough observes that validity is not so much a property of a test as it is a matter of how well it succeeds at its intended use. A comparison of the two approaches and their implications could make a useful and interesting lecture topic.

DISCUSSION QUESTIONS

1. In what ways is the psychology of today's college students different from that of your parents? Do you think differently than they do? Would the conclusions of research done with college students also apply to their parents? Can you think of any particular areas where they would be most likely to be different?

2. Will research done on college students also be relevant to members of ethnic minorities or to people who live in other cultures? In what areas would you expect to find the most differences?

3. (Students who have taken statistics only) What does a significance level tell you? What does it omit? If we don't use significance to decide if our results mean anything, what can we use instead?

4. Is deception in psychological research justified? Does it depend on the research question? Does it depend on the specific kind of deception? Who if anybody is harmed by the use of deception in research?

5. (Careful with this one) Some psychologists do research on differences between races in intelligence. Let's say members of one race really do have higher IQ scores than members of another. Should we do research to find this out? Or is this issue better left alone? Once the research is done, what would such a result mean? How would it be used?

6. Repeat question 5, but substitute *gender* for *race*.

MULTIPLE-CHOICE QUESTIONS

1. According to the text, scientific education is intended
   a. to teach what is known and how to find out what is not yet known.
   b. to convey what is known about a subject so it can be applied.
   c. to train individuals in the manufacture of machines and tools.
   d. all of the above.

   Answer: a   Pages: 41–42
   Topic: Scientific Education and Technical Training

2. A _____ would receive technical training while a _____
   would receive scientific education.
   a. pharmacologist; pharmacist
   b. physician; biologist
   c. computer scientist; botanist
   d. research psychologist; clinical psychologist

   Answer: b   Page: 42
   Topic: Scientific Education and Technical Training

3. The effects of irrelevant influences that might tend to lessen your ability to
   see the trait or state you are trying to measure are called
   a. measurement error.
   b. hypothetical constructs.
   c. aggregating variables.
   d. psychometrics.

   Answer: a   Page: 42
   Topic: Quality of Data—Reliability

4. If you can get the same measurement repeatedly, then your measurement is
   a. reliable.
   b. valid.
   c. significant.
   d. generalizable.

   Answer: a   Page: 43
   Topic: Quality of Data—Reliability

5. A method or instrument that provides the same comparative information
   repeatedly is
   a. valid.
   b. reliable.

c. significant.
d. generalizable.

Answer: b   Page: 43
Topic: Quality of Data—Reliability

6. One can increase the reliability of a personality test by
    a. aggregating.
    b. measuring something important.
    c. being careful and using uniform procedures.
    d. all of the above.

Answer: d   Page: 44
Topic: Quality of Data—Reliability

7. The most important and generally useful way to enhance reliability is to
    a. minimize error variance.
    b. measure something that is important.
    c. aggregate your measurements.
    d. maximize error variance.

Answer: c   Page: 44
Topic: Quality of Data—Reliability

8. On Friday, Terence completes the Self-Monitoring Scale and receives a score of 49. On the following Tuesday, he fills out the scale again and receives a score of 28. Terence's scores on the Self-Monitoring Scale do not appear to be
    a. valid.
    b. reliable.
    c. significant.
    d. psychometrics.

Answer: b   Page: 44
Topic: Quality of Data—Reliability

9. Validity is the degree to which a measurement
    a. is consistent and stable.
    b. if repeated, provides the same result.
    c. actually reflects or measures what you think it does.
    d. is reliable.

Answer: c   Page: 45
Topic: Quality of Data—Validity

10. Jane recently completed the ACME Intelligence Test, a new test that is designed to measure her IQ. She took the test twice and each time received an IQ score of 130, which the test administrator told her indicates that she is extremely intelligent. However, when Jane completed the Stanford-Binet and the WAIS (two well-established intelligence tests) last month, she scored in the low 70s, indicating that she has an IQ that is well below average. It appears that the ACME Intelligence Scale may be a
    a. valid measure of intelligence.
    b. valid but unreliable measure of intelligence.
    c. reliable but not valid measure of intelligence.
    d. more accurate measure of intelligence than the Stanford-Binet or the WAIS.

    Answer: c   Page: 45
    Topic: Quality of Data—Validity

11. Reliability is _____ condition for validity.
    a. a necessary and sufficient
    b. a necessary but not sufficient
    c. an unnecessary but sufficient
    d. none of the above

    Answer: b   Page: 45
    Topic: Quality of Data—Validity

12. A research strategy that involves gathering as many different measurements as you can of a construct and determining if they are correlated is called
    a. construct validation.
    b. aggregation.
    c. generalization.
    d. internal validation.

    Answer: a   Page: 46
    Topic: Quality of Data—Validity

13. Reliability and validity are both aspects of a broader concept called
    a. aggregation.
    b. experimental differentiation.
    c. construct validity.
    d. generalizability.

    Answer: d   Page: 47
    Topic: Quality of Data—Generalizability

14. Many researchers, for purposes of convenience, study the behavior of college students and then assume that what they learn applies to people in general. This practice severely limits
    a. the ecological reliability of their research.
    b. the internal validity of their studies.
    c. the generalizability over participants.
    d. a and b.

    Answer: c   Pages: 47–48
    Topic: Quality of Data—Generalizability

15. Which of the following sampling methods affords a researcher the greatest generalizability?
    a. Randomly selecting introductory psychology students to participate
    b. Randomly selecting both high school and college students to participate
    c. Recruiting all the executives at a large Fortune 500 company to participate
    d. Using a random telephone number dial system to select study participants

    Answer: d   Pages: 47–48
    Topic: Quality of Data—Generalizability

16. The tendency of a group of people who lived at a particular time to be different in some way from those who lived earlier or later is called by psychologists
    a. a generational disparity.
    b. a cohort effect.
    c. the generation gap.
    d. age diversity.

    Answer: b   Pages: 49–50
    Topic: Quality of Data—Generalizability

17. Dr. Jones measures aggression by counting the number of times a research participant hits an inflatable "Bobo doll." If this is the only way Dr. Jones measures aggression, the results of his study may lack
    a. stimulus reliability.
    b. generalizability over responses.
    c. predictive validity.
    d. domain specificity.

    Answer: b   Page: 51
    Topic: Quality of Data—Generalizability

18. Egon Brunswik's concept that research should be designed to sample across all of the domains to which the investigator will wish to apply the results is referred to as
    a. generalizability over subjects.
    b. representative design.
    c. ecological reliability.
    d. domain sampling.

    Answer: b   Pages: 51–52
    Topic: Quality of Data—Generalizability

19. Dr. Leslie is interested in studying the relationship between mood and willingness to help a stranger. She randomly assigns half of her subjects to the good-mood group and shows them funny film clips to induce a good mood. The other half of her subjects are assigned to the bad-mood group and watch boring and unpleasant film clips to induce a bad mood. She then gives every subject an opportunity to donate money to a homeless stranger and measures the amount of money they donate. Dr. Leslie is using
    a. an experimental design.
    b. a correlational design.
    c. a case study design.
    d. a repeated measures design.

    Answer: a   Pages: 52–57
    Topic: Correlational and Experimental Designs

20. Dr. Leslie is interested in studying the relationship between mood and willingness to help a stranger. Every participant in her study completes a mood-rating questionnaire, describing his or her current mood. She then gives every subject an opportunity to donate money to a homeless stranger and measures the amount of money he or she donates. Dr. Leslie is using
    a. an experimental design.
    b. a correlational design.
    c. a case study design.
    d. a repeated measures design.

    Answer: b   Pages: 52–57
    Topic: Correlational and Experimental Designs

21. A disadvantage of the experimental method is
    a. that it can create levels of a variable that are unlikely or impossible in real life.
    b. that experiments cannot be done on some research questions, for ethical or other reasons.

c. that the researcher can never be sure what he or she is manipulating and where the causality is located.

d. all of the above.

Answer: d   Pages: 56–57
Topic: Correlational and Experimental Designs

22. According to the text, the only difference between the experimental and correlational methods is that in the experimental method the presumably causal variable is _____ whereas in the correlational method the same variable is _____.
a. externally derived; internally derived
b. significant; important
c. manipulated; measured
d. reliable; valid

Answer: c   Page: 55
Topic: Correlational and Experimental Designs

23. The most touted advantage of the experimental method is
a. that it allows the assessment of causality.
b. that it allows the study of naturally occurring individual differences that already exist in the participants.
c. that subjects are always randomly sampled from the general population.
d. all of the above.

Answer: a   Page: 56
Topic: Correlational and Experimental Designs

24. If a psychologist describes a research result as significant, it means that the result
a. is important.
b. is large and dramatic.
c. was unlikely to have occurred by chance.
d. will likely revolutionize the field.

Answer: c   Pages: 57–58
Topic: Correlational and Experimental Designs

25. A number between –1 and +1 that indexes the association between any two variables is called
a. a significance level.
b. the probability value.

c. the variation index.

d. a correlation coefficient.

Answer: d   Page: 60
Topic: Correlational and Experimental Designs

26. If test scores go down as anxiety goes up, then
    a. test scores and anxiety are positively correlated.
    b. test scores and anxiety are negatively correlated.
    c. test scores and anxiety are unrelated.
    d. the correlation between test scores and anxiety is +1.0.

Answer: b   Page: 60
Topic: Correlational and Experimental Designs

27. Using the Binomial Effect Size Display, if there is a correlation of +.30 between drinking (or not drinking) alcohol before driving and the likelihood of having (or avoiding) a car accident, then out of one hundred people who drink you would expect _____ of them to have an accident.
    a. one hundred
    b. sixty
    c. ninety
    d. sixty-five

Answer: d   Page: 62
Topic: Correlational and Experimental Designs

28. Assume that you are studying 200 subjects, all of whom are sick. An experimental drug is given to 100 of them; the other 100 are given nothing. If the correlation between taking the drug (or not), and living (or dying), is +.26, then _____ of those who got the drug would still be alive at the end of the study.
    a. 13 percent
    b. 63 percent
    c. 26 percent
    d. 52 percent

Answer: b   Page: 62
Topic: Correlational and Experimental Designs

29. The Binomial Effect Size Display is a method for illustrating
    a. heritabilities.
    b. validity coefficients.

c. effect sizes.

d. personality coefficients.

Answer: c   Page: 62
Topic: Correlational and Experimental Designs

30. Linda is taking an intelligence test in a classroom on Thursday afternoon.
During the test, the teachers walk through the halls and chat with each
other, and their chatting distracts Linda from concentrating on her test.
Due to these distractions, Linda scores lower on the test than she would
have if she had been able to concentrate fully and perform up to her true
potential. The influence of the teachers' chatting is an example of
a. reliability.
b. a validity bias.
c. a cohort effect.
d. measurement error.

Answer: d   Page: 42
Topic: Quality of Data—Reliability

31. According to Cronbach and Meehl's (1955) terminology, psychological
attributes like intelligence and sociability are examples of _____,
while an IQ test or a questionnaire about sociability are examples of
specific tests or measurements.
a. constructs
b. validity
c. L data
d. ecological variables

Answer: a   Page: 45
Topic: Quality of Data—Validity

32. Dr. Grant studies shyness. To measure shyness, she asks participants to
rate, on a scale of 1 to 10, how nervous they get when meeting strangers.
Her colleague, Dr. Ludwig, suggests that Dr. Grant may want to include
more than one question in her assessment and then get the average ratings
across all the questions she asks. Dr. Ludwig tells Dr. Grant that this would
probably lead to a more reliable measurement of shyness. Dr. Ludwig's
suggestion is an example of which principle of measurement?
a. Strong effect size
b. Experimental design
c. Aggregation
d. Construct validity

Answer: c   Page: 44
Topic: Quality of Data—Reliability

33. The fact that most modern empirical research in psychology has been based on white, middle-class sophomores may reduce the _____ of psychological research.
    a. reliability
    b. generalizability
    c. cohort effects
    d. statistical significance

    Answer: b   Page: 50
    Topic: Quality of Data—Reliability

CHAPTER 4 | Personality Traits and Behavior

OUTLINE

SUMMARY

The trait approach to personality begins by assuming that individuals differ in their characteristic patterns of thought, feeling, and behavior. These patterns are called personality traits. Classifying people in this way raises an important problem, however: people are inconsistent. Indeed, it has been suggested by some psychologists that people are so inconsistent in their behavior from one situation to the next that it is not worthwhile to try to characterize them in terms of personality traits. The debate among psychologists over this issue was called the consistency controversy. Opponents of the trait approach argue that a review of the personality literature reveals that the ability of traits to predict behavior is extremely limited, that situations are therefore more important than personality traits for determining what people do, and that not only is personality assessment (the measurement of traits) a waste of time but also many of our intuitions about each other are fundamentally wrong.

The responses to the first of these arguments are that a fair review of the literature reveals that the predictability of behavior from traits is better than is sometimes acknowledged, that better research methods can make this predictability even higher, and that the upper limit for predictability (a correlation of about .40) is bigger than sometimes recognized. The response to the second of these arguments is that many important effects of situations on behavior are no bigger, statistically, than the documented size of the effects of personality traits on behavior. If the responses to the first two criticisms are valid, then the third, that assessment and our intuitions are both fundamentally flawed, falls of its own weight. The many personality trait terms in our language give support to the importance of traits, which provide a useful way to predict behavior and understand personality.

ABOUT THE CHAPTER

A fundamental first issue for personality psychology is, does personality even exist? This is an important issue quite aside from the consistency controversy that occupied the attention of many personality psychologists for about two decades (1968–1988). This chapter reviews the consistency controversy and the arguments on both sides.

I was one of the protagonists in this controversy, on the pro-trait side, so it should not be surprising that this chapter basically concludes that Mischel and his critique of personality were mistaken. However, I also explain that the criticism was good for the field because it forced personality psychology to rethink some of its basic assumptions.

TEACHING NOTES

The trick in teaching this material is not to turn off the students by making the consistency controversy seem like the typical academic tempest in a teapot. It is important to avoid the "he said/did not say" tone of so much of the professional literature, when the debate often got bogged down in a close reading of comments that Mischel would or would not acknowledge having made. Rather, the focus needs to be kept on the broader issue, which is: In what sense do consistent personality traits exist? This is a question that is interesting and important regardless of what Mischelians and anti-Mischelians do or do not believe about it and would be interesting and important even if Mischel had never written his famous critique.

Ever since I first taught the personality course, I have regularly included lectures on the person-situation debate. For the first several years I did three lectures, then two, then one. Recently, for the first time, I have omitted this topic from my lectures even though it remains in the text. Perhaps the controversy is over, and in a short personality course where choices must be made (I teach on the ten-week quarter system), this is one topic an instructor could safely skip over. On the other hand, the basic issue remains important and many of the substantive and methodological issues raised by the controversy can be helpful in framing discussions of topics that arise later in the course.

PIECES OF THE PERSONALITY PUZZLE

Three selections in Part II of the reader are directly relevant to this chapter: the excerpt from Mischel's famous book, the brief rebuttal by Block, and the historical overview of the controversy by Kenrick and Funder. It can also be noted that the Allport selection, which dates from the 1930s, anticipates and rebuts several of the criticisms made by Mischel 30 years later.

DISCUSSION QUESTIONS

1. What are the most consistent aspects of the personalities of the people you know? What are the most inconsistent aspects?

2. Do you use personality traits when describing yourself or other people? Are you fooling yourself when you do so?

3. Have you ever had somebody else misunderstand your personality by thinking your behavior is more consistent than it really is?

4. Next time you talk with your parents, explain the consistency issue to them and ask them if they think people have consistent personality traits. Then do the same with college friends who have not taken this course. Are their answers different? How?

MULTIPLE-CHOICE QUESTIONS

1. An ultimate criterion for any measurement of a personality trait is whether it
   a. makes the trait easy to understand.
   b. can be used to predict behavior.
   c. can be used to measure gender differences.
   d. is based on ordinary language.

   Answer: b   Page: 71
   Topic: Personality Traits and Behavior

2. The trait approach focuses exclusively on
   a. the measurement of absolute levels of traits.
   b. traits that all people have in common.
   c. unique aspects of each individual.
   d. comparative individual differences.

   Answer: d   Page: 71
   Topic: Personality Traits and Behavior

3. One criticism of the trait approach is that it
   a. ignores the trait terms of everyday language.
   b. does not focus on individual differences.
   c. ignores what all people have in common.
   d. exaggerates the effects that situations have on behavior.

   Answer: c   Page: 72
   Topic: The Measurement of Individual Differences

4. The trait approach is based on empirical research
   a. that is mostly correlational in nature.
   b. that is mostly experimental in nature.
   c. from case studies.
   d. from archival studies.

   Answer: a   Page: 71
   Topic: The Measurement of Individual Differences

5. According to Kluckhohn and Murray, "Every man is in certain respects
   (a) like all other men, (b) like some other men, (c) like no other man."
   Which section of this quote most closely reflects what trait psychologists
   study?
   a. "Like all other men"
   b. "Like some other men"
   c. "Like no other man"
   d. All of the above

   Answer: b   Page: 73
   Topic: The Measurement of Individual Differences

6. A fundamental problem for the trait approach is that
   a. individual differences cannot be measured reliably.
   b. situations do not affect behavior.
   c. people are inconsistent.
   d. correlational methods do not provide ready indices of effect size.

   Answer: c   Page: 73
   Topic: People Are Inconsistent

7. Walter Mischel and his 1968 book, *Personality and Assessment,* are of historical importance because Mischel
   a. provided the most cogent argument for why trait theory and psychodynamic theory should be integrated.
   b. is credited with starting the person-situation debate by claiming that personality is not as important as situational factors in behavioral prediction.
   c. provided the first real defense of trait theory against the situationist attack.
   d. is the first modern researcher to begin to scientifically validate some of Freud's claims about the unconscious.

   Answer: b   Page: 75
   Topic: The Person-Situation Debate

8. In his book, *Personality and Assessment,* Walter Mischel argued that
   a. traits are the only factors that influence human behavior.
   b. situations do not reliably predict consistent behavioral trends.
   c. behavior is too inconsistent to allow individual differences to be characterized in terms of broad personality traits.
   d. personality traits transcend the immediate situation and moment and provide the most consistent guide to a person's actions.

   Answer: c   Page: 75
   Topic: The Person-Situation Debate

9. The situationist argument, as presented in Mischel's *Personality and Assessment,* holds
   a. that a thorough review of the literature reveals that there is a limit to how well one can predict behavior from personality.
   b. that situations are more important than personality traits for determining behavior.
   c. that our everyday intuitions about people are fundamentally flawed.
   d. all of the above.

   Answer: d   Page: 76
   Topic: The Person-Situation Debate

10. Walter Mischel, in his book *Personality and Assessment,* argued that behavior is best predicted from
    a. situations.
    b. personality variables.
    c. motivations.
    d. goals.

    Answer: a   Page: 76
    Topic: The Person-Situation Debate

11. Situationism is the position that
    a. situations do not influence behavior.
    b. situations are more important than personality traits in determining behavior.
    c. the ability of personality traits to predict behavior is severely limited.
    d. b and c.

    Answer: d   Page: 77
    Topic: The Person-Situation Debate

12. The behavioral measurements used in the studies reviewed by Mischel were
    a. most frequently taken from real-life settings.
    b. nearly all gathered in laboratory settings.
    c. garnered from clinicians' case studies.
    d. archival data.

    Answer: b   Page: 77
    Topic: The Person-Situation Debate

13. A correlation coefficient is _____ that ranges between
    _____.
    a. an effect size; .30 and .40
    b. a probability; 1 and 100
    c. an effect size; −1 and +1
    d. a significance test; zero and infinity

    Answer: c   Page: 77
    Topic: The Person-Situation Debate

14. If there is a positive correlation between extraversion and risk taking, then the
    a. researcher can be certain that extraversion causes risk taking.
    b. higher a person's extraversion score, the more risks he or she is likely to take.
    c. lower a person's extraversion score, the more risks he or she is likely to take.
    d. researcher can be certain that extraversion and risk taking are unrelated.

    Answer: b   Page: 77
    Topic: The Person-Situation Debate

15. According to situationists, the upper limit of personality coefficients is estimated as
    a. .30 to .40.
    b. 1 to 100.

c. −1 to +1.

d. zero to infinity.

Answer: a   Page: 78
Topic: The Person-Situation Debate

16. The Mischelian argument is that correlations between personality and behavior or between behavior in one situation and behavior in another
    a. are usually between .50 and .60.
    b. are essentially zero.
    c. are large and important.
    d. seldom exceed .30 or .40.

Answer: d   Page: 77
Topic: The Person-Situation Debate

17. One kind of research improvement offered in response to the situationist critique suggests identifying those individuals whose behavior is more consistent than others. This research improvement involves
    a. aggregating multiple measurements.
    b. using a moderator variable approach.
    c. employing the BESD.
    d. predicting actions at particular moments rather than general behavioral trends.

Answer: b   Page: 79
Topic: The Person-Situation Debate

18. Which of the following behaviors would be the easiest to predict accurately?
    a. Mary will smile at ten tomorrow morning.
    b. At a party on Friday, Susan will talk to at least ten people.
    c. David will generally be on time for work next week.
    d. None of the above. Each of these behaviors would be easy to predict.

Answer: c   Page: 80
Topic: The Person-Situation Debate

19. Which of the following behaviors would tend to be consistent across situations?
    a. Speaking loudly
    b. Trying to impress someone
    c. Dominating another person
    d. Cooperating with teammates

Answer: a   Page: 80
Topic: The Person-Situation Debate

20. Which of the following would be an example of using a moderator variable approach to improve the predictability of behavior from personality?
    a. Measuring how frequently you are late to work using a daily diary report of your everyday behavior
    b. Collecting information about your responses in stressful work situations
    c. Trying to predict how warm and friendly you will act when you meet your new in-laws next Monday
    d. Determining if the behavior of high self-monitors is less consistent than that of low self-monitors

    Answer: d   Page: 80
    Topic: The Person-Situation Debate

21. In order to improve personality research, researchers can
    a. check for moderator variables.
    b. predict behavioral trends rather than single acts.
    c. measure behavior in real life.
    d. all of the above.

    Answer: d   Page: 80
    Topic: The Person-Situation Debate

22. One difficulty with the moderator variable approach is that
    a. no potential moderators have yet to be identified by researchers.
    b. many direct behavioral measurements must be taken.
    c. real-life behaviors are not easy to assess.
    d. moderator variables are subtle and difficult to measure.

    Answer: d   Page: 80
    Topic: The Person-Situation Debate

23. Traditionally, the usual practice to evaluate the degree to which behavior is affected by the situation has been to
    a. square the correlation coefficient for the relationship between behavior and some aspect of the situation.
    b. determine the percentage of variance accounted for by personality, subtract that from 100 percent, and then assign the remaining percentage of the variance, by default, to the situation.
    c. add the variance in the behavioral measure to the variance for the situational variable.
    d. use the correlation coefficient for the relationship between the behavioral measure and the situational variable an indicator of effect size.

    Answer: b   Page: 82
    Topic: The Person-Situation Debate

24. Historically, to evaluate the effects of personality variables, personality psychologists have concentrated on _____. To evaluate the effects of situational variables, social psychologists have concentrated on _____.
   a. variance; standard deviations
   b. standard deviations; variance
   c. effect size; statistical significance
   d. statistical significance; effect size

   Answer: c   Page: 84
   Topic: The Person-Situation Debate

25. Funder and Ozer (1983) examined the results of three classic social psychological studies. They converted the results to effect sizes and found that the effects were typically equivalent to correlations in the range of _____.
   a. .10 to .20
   b. .30 to .40
   c. .61 to .75
   d. .70 to .97

   Answer: b   Pages: 84–85
   Topic: The Person-Situation Debate

26. Funder and Ozer (1983) converted the results of three classic social psychological studies to effect sizes. After comparing those effect sizes with those typically obtained by personality psychologists, Funder and Ozer concluded that
   a. situational variables, like personality variables, cannot predict behavior.
   b. both situational and personality variables are important determinants of behavior.
   c. the upper limit for a situation coefficient is only .20.
   d. the three studies were so fundamentally flawed that they don't allow us to conclude anything about the predictability of behavior from situational variables.

   Answer: b   Page: 85
   Topic: The Person-Situation Debate

27. According to the text, the most plausible explanation for the 17.953 trait terms found by Allport and Odbert (1936) is that
   a. we need ways to describe important psychological differences among people.
   b. their methodology was biased toward finding many terms.

    c. trait terms are essentially redundant because we have many different words for the same small set of traits.

    d. we simply make up differences between the personalities of people who we know and assign words to describe these perceived differences.

Answer: a   Page: 86
Topic: The Person-Situation Debate

28. The large number of trait terms in the English language indicates that
    a. we need them to discriminate between different types of people.
    b. personality traits are an important part of our culture.
    c. when it comes to personality, one size does not fit all.
    d. all of the above.

Answer: d   Page: 86
Topic: The Person-Situation Debate

29. A review of the research on the predictability of behavior from personality traits indicates that
    a. behavior can never be reliably predicted from personality variables.
    b. the predictability of behavior from personality is better than is sometimes acknowledged.
    c. the predictability of behavior from situations is worse than the predictability from personality.
    d. Mischel was right.

Answer: b   Page: 88
Topic: The Person-Situation Debate

30. Mischel's arguments concerning traits, situations, and behavior were based on
    a. a short and selective review of generally poorly conducted studies.
    b. a detailed review of generally high-quality research.
    c. research that showed support for the trait perspective *and* the situationist perspective.
    d. b and c.

Answer: a   Page: 78
Topic: The Person-Situation Debate

CHAPTER 5 | Personality Assessment I: Personality Testing and Its Consequences

SUMMARY

Any characteristic pattern of behavior, thought, and emotional experience that exhibits relative consistency across time and situations is part of an individual's personality. These patterns include personality traits as well as such psychological attributes as goals, moods, and strategies. Personality assessment is a frequent activity of industrial and clinical psychologists and researchers. Everybody also performs personality assessments of the people they know in daily life. An important issue for assessments, whether by psychologists or by laypersons, is the degree to which those assessments are correct. This chapter examined how psychologists' personality tests are constructed and validated. Some personality tests comprise S data and others comprise B data, but a more commonly drawn distinction is between projective tests and objective tests. Projective tests try to gain insight into personality by presenting participants with ambiguous stimuli, and recording how the participants respond. Objective tests ask participants specific questions and assess personality on the basis of how the participants answer. Objective tests can be constructed by rational, factor analytic, or empirical methods, and the modern practice is to use a combination of all three methods. Some people are uncomfortable with the practice of personality assessment because they see it as an unfair invasion of privacy. However, because people inevitably judge each others' personalities, the real issue is how personality assessment should be done—through informal intuitions or more-formalized techniques.

ABOUT THE CHAPTER

Most of this chapter is a straightforward exposition of the methods of constructing and evaluating personality tests. It includes some recent developments, including legal troubles that users of the MMPI have experienced. The chapter concludes with a discussion of the ethics of personality testing.

TEACHING NOTES

I have found that students are more interested in this material if illustrations of actual personality tests are employed as often as possible. For example, it is an entertaining and useful exercise to show students Rorschach ink blots or TAT pictures and have them write their responses. You can have them write their reponses anonymously, then exchange them randomly, and then try to evaluate the meaning of the responses they are given. Many self-report personality tests can be administered in a classroom setting as well.

My favorite for this purpose is the Self-monitoring Scale. Sometimes I have students complete this test before reading any of the material in Chapters 4 to 7. The nice thing about this scale is that the property it was designed to measure is interesting but nonthreatening. Nobody is likely to be traumatized by his or her self-monitoring score; nearly everybody seems to get the score they would desire (i.e., high self-monitors *want* to be high self-monitors).

The ethics of personality testing can trigger interesting and useful discussions. First, it is important to remind students not to be swept away by the technology, impressive appearance, and interest value of personality tests. They still are of limited validity, and even though many are valid enough to be useful, none are perfect. In particular, I warn my students that if they ever take a personality test that tells them something about themselves they believe to be untrue, the odds are at least 90-10 that they are right and the test is wrong. Students should also be warned about the Barnum effect—that people usually find generally worded personality descriptions of themselves persuasive, even when everybody is given the same description.

PIECES OF THE PERSONALITY PUZZLE

The relevant sections of the reader are the O'Connor and Allport selections in Part II, which in different ways define what trait assessment is all about.

DISCUSSION QUESTIONS

1. If you wanted to understand someone's personality, and could only ask three questions, what would those questions be? What traits would the answers reveal?

2. How would you choose somebody to be your roommate? Your employee? A date? Would personality traits be relevant to your choice? How would you try to evaluate those traits?

3. Have you ever taken a personality test? Did the results seem accurate? Were the results useful?

4. How many uses can you think of for knowing somebody's personality test score? Are any (or all) of these uses unethical?

MULTIPLE-CHOICE QUESTIONS

1. Personality assessment refers to
   a. a plan designed to treat personality disorders.
   b. the analysis and interpretation of genetic markers of personality.
   c. the measurement of any characteristic pattern of behavior, thought, or emotion.
   d. the selection of a group of individuals with the most unique temperaments.

   Answer: c   Page: 90
   Topic: The Nature of Personality Assessment

2. When professional personality judgments are evaluated, it is typically said that we are evaluating their _____; when amateur personality judgments are evaluated, it is typically said that we are evaluating their

   _____.

a. accuracy; validity
b. validity; accuracy
c. reliability; validity
d. agreement; significance

Answer: b   Page: 90
Topic: The Nature of Personality Assessment

3. The two basic criteria for evaluating the validity of a personality judgment are
   a. rationality and empiricism.
   b. usefulness and practicality.
   c. agreement and behavioral prediction.
   d. consensus and ability to generate testable hypotheses.

Answer: c   Page: 90
Topic: The Nature of Personality Assessment

4. The MMPI was designed to
   a. clinically assess individuals with psychological disorders.
   b. assess nondisturbed individuals.
   c. identify the Big Five personality factors.
   d. measure integrity in job candidates.

Answer: a   Page: 92
Topic: Personality Tests

5. The California Psychological Inventory was designed to
   a. clinically assess individuals with psychological disorders.
   b. assess nondisturbed individuals.
   c. identify the Big Five personality factors.
   d. measure integrity in job candidates.

Answer: b   Page: 92
Topic: Personality Tests

6. Your responses to the item "I am an intelligent person" would be
   _____ while your score on an intelligence test that reflects the number of problems you got right would be _____.
   a. B data; L data
   b. S data; L data
   c. I data; B data
   d. S data; B data

Answer: d   Page: 93
Topic: Personality Tests

7. When taking a(n) _____, a person interprets a meaningless, ambiguous stimulus in order to access the inner workings of his or her mind.
   a. rationally constructed test
   b. projective test
   c. factor analytic test
   d. objective test

   Answer: b   Page: 93
   Topic: Personality Tests—Projective Tests

8. All projective tests
   a. involve stimuli with no clear meaning.
   b. involve the construction of stories and narratives.
   c. require choosing among multiple, predetermined alternatives.
   d. rely on computer scoring methods.

   Answer: a   Page: 93
   Topic: Personality Tests—Projective Tests

9. If you were shown an inkblot and asked to describe what you saw, you would be taking the
   a. MMPI.
   b. CPI.
   c. Rorschach test.
   d. Thematic Apperception Test.

   Answer: c   Page: 94
   Topic: Personality Tests—Projective Tests

10. A psychologist administering the Thematic Apperception Test (TAT) asks respondents to
    a. draw a person so that she may determine which parts are left out or exaggerated.
    b. describe their current level of hostility so that she can measure their Type A tendencies.
    c. tell stories about pictures she shows them to assess their motivational state.
    d. describe their perceptions of the causes of people's behavior so that she can measure attributional complexity.

    Answer: c   Page: 94
    Topic: Personality Tests—Projective Tests

11. Which projective test appears to have evidence that comes close to establishing its validity?
    a. Draw-a-Person Test
    b. Thematic Apperception Test (TAT)

c. Rorschach test
d. b and c

Answer: d   Pages: 94–95
Topic: Personality Tests—Projective Tests

12. One problem with projective tests is
    a. that two different interpreters of the same response might come to different conclusions about the scoring and meaning of the response.
    b. that they are relatively inefficient and expensive.
    c. that although the items discriminate between groups, the content of the items may seem contrary or absurd to test takers.
    d. a and b.

Answer: d   Page: 95
Topic: Personality Tests—Projective Tests

13. If a test consists of a list of true/false questions and is graded using a computer-scorable answer sheet, then it is
    a. a projective test.
    b. a Q-sort.
    c. an objective test.
    d. a commonality scale.

Answer: c   Page: 96
Topic: Personality Tests—Objective Tests

14. If everybody read, interpreted, and answered an item in exactly the same way, then that item would
    a. not be very useful for the assessment of individual differences.
    b. be very informative about personality.
    c. have been developed using the rational method of test construction.
    d. be empirically derived.

Answer: a   Page: 97
Topic: Personality Tests—Objective Tests

15. The commonality scale on the CPI is
    a. used to identify individuals who are deliberately attempting to sabotage a test.
    b. used to detect illiterates who are pretending to know how to read.
    c. a subset of items that are answered in the same way by at least 95 percent of all people.
    d. all of the above.

Answer: d   Page: 97
Topic: Personality Tests—Objective Tests

16. The reason that objective tests include so many items is to increase
    a. the rationality of the test.
    b. the reliability of the test.
    c. the validity of the test.
    d. a and b.

    Answer: d   Page: 98
    Topic: Personality Tests—Objective Tests

17. Dr. Akita is designing a test to measure sociability. She writes items that seem directly and obviously related to sociability, such as "I like to go to parties" or "I enjoy the company of other people." Which method of test construction is Dr. Akita using?
    a. Empirical method
    b. Factor analytic method
    c. Rational method
    d. Projective method

    Answer: c   Page: 98
    Topic: Methods of Objective Test Construction

18. The basis of the _____ method of test construction is to come up with items that seem directly, obviously, and logically related to what it is you wish to measure.
    a. rational
    b. empirical
    c. philosophical
    d. factor analytic

    Answer: a   Page: 98
    Topic: Methods of Objective Test Construction

19. For any rationally constructed personality scale to work, it must satisfy which of the following conditions?
    a. The items on the form must all be valid indicators of what the tester is trying to measure.
    b. The person who completes the form must be able and willing to accurately report his or her self-assessment.
    c. Each item must mean the same thing to the person who fills out the form as it did to the psychologist who wrote it.
    d. All of the above.

    Answer: d   Pages: 99–100
    Topic: Methods of Objective Test Construction

20. Tests developed using _____ methods of test construction are currently the most common form of psychological measurement device.
    a. factor analytic
    b. rational
    c. empirical
    d. a combination of

    Answer: b   Page: 100
    Topic: Methods of Objective Test Construction

21. The factor analytic technique is designed to
    a. identify individuals who are attempting to lie or sabotage a test.
    b. identify groups of test items that seem to be alike.
    c. identify items that mean the same thing to the respondent as they do to the researcher.
    d. analyze and score responses to projective tests.

    Answer: b   Page: 101
    Topic: Methods of Objective Test Construction

22. The approach to personality-test construction that examines a set of correlations among many items to identify items that are highly correlated is called the _____ approach.
    a. nomothetic
    b. idiographic
    c. rational
    d. factor analytic

    Answer: d   Page: 102
    Topic: Methods of Objective Test Construction

23. Currently, an emerging consensus among personality researchers is that there are _____ fundamental personality traits.
    a. three
    b. five
    c. sixteen
    d. twenty

    Answer: b   Page: 103
    Topic: Methods of Objective Test Construction

24. Which of the following is *not* a limitation of the factor analytic approach?
    a. Sometimes the factors that emerge do not make sense.
    b. The results are only as good as the items that go into it.

  c. The factors are only as good as the criterion groups on which they are based.

  d. It is up to psychologists to decide what the factors mean.

Answer: c   Pages: 103–104
Topic: Methods of Objective Test Construction

25. The Big Five are
  a. Freudian psychoanalytic stages of personality development.
  b. steps in the construction of empirical tests.
  c. factor analytically derived dimensions of personality.
  d. the primary methods of test construction used by personality psychologists.

Answer: c   Page: 103
Topic: Methods of Objective Test Construction

26. The sole basis by which items are selected for empirically derived personality scales is whether
  a. their content adequately reflects the construct to be measured.
  b. they are correlated with other items on the scales.
  c. the respondent will be willing and able to truthfully give an accurate self-assessment for them.
  d. they are answered differently by different kinds of people.

Answer: d   Page: 105
Topic: Methods of Objective Test Construction

27. Faking responses in order to influence test results is most difficult on _____ constructed tests.
  a. factor analytically
  b. empirically
  c. rationally
  d. nomothetically

Answer: b   Page: 106
Topic: Methods of Objective Test Construction

28. If you developed a personality test without even looking at the item content, you would probably be using a(n) _____ method of test construction
  a. factor analytic
  b. rational
  c. projective
  d. empirical

Answer: d   Page: 106
Topic: Methods of Objective Test Construction

29. Integrity tests administered in preemployment screening provide good measures of
    a. conscientiousness.
    b. intelligence.
    c. drug use on the job.
    d. sociability.

    Answer: a   Page: 110
    Topic: Purposes of Personality Testing

30. One objection to the use of vocational interest tests is that these tests
    a. measure conscientiousness rather than vocational interest.
    b. may prevent women or minority group members from joining certain fields.
    c. measure performance ability rather than job interest.
    d. can be used to tell individuals what kind of occupational group they most resemble.

    Answer: b   Page: 110
    Topic: Purposes of Personality Testing

31. One conclusion that has been made about testing is that eliminating the use of personality tests in employment screening will
    a. prevent biases from affecting hiring decisions.
    b. decrease the likelihood that women and minorities will be discriminated against in hiring.
    c. increase the use of lie detector tests and drug tests in employment screening.
    d. not prevent traits from being judged but will change how they will be judged.

    Answer: d   Page: 112
    Topic: Purposes of Personality Testing

32. Imagine that you wanted to develop a test to measure depression. You gathered a set of one hundred potential test items and asked a sample of people with clinical depression and a sample of nondepressed people to respond to the items. For your final version of the test, you decided to keep only the fifteen items that the depressed and nondepressed groups answered differently. You would be using _____ method of test construction.
    a. a factor analytic
    b. a rational
    c. a projective
    d. an empirical

    Answer: d   Page: 105
    Topic: Personality Tests—Objective Tests

CHAPTER 6

Personality Assessment II: Personality Judgment in Daily Life

SUMMARY

People judge the personalities of each other and of themselves all the time, and these judgments often have important consequences. The judgments of others can affect your opportunities and can create self-fulfilling prophecies, or expectancy effects. Your judgments of yourself influence what you are likely to attempt to accomplish in life. Therefore, it is important to examine when and how judgments of the self and of others are accurate. Recent research evaluates the accuracy of personality judgment in terms of agreement and predictive validity. That is, judgments that agree with judgments from other sources (such as other people) or that are able to predict the people judged are deemed more likely to be accurate than judgments that do not agree with each other or that cannot predict behavior. Research has examined four kinds of variables that seem to affect the likelihood of accurate personality judgment: (1) the good judge, or the possibility that some judges are more accurate than others; (2) the good target, or the possibility that some individuals are easier to judge than others; (3) the good trait, or the possibility that some traits are easier to judge accurately than others; and (4) good information, or the possiblity that more or better information about the target makes accurate judgment more likely. This research leads to a model of the process of accurate personality judgment that describes it as a function of the relevance, availability, detection, and utilization of behavioral cues.

ABOUT THE CHAPTER

The most important point of this chapter is that personality assessment is not something done only by personality psychologists. Everybody does it in daily life. And the very same criteria by which one would evaluate the validity of a personality test can and should be applied to evaluating the accuracy of a personality judgment. This is the place where personality psychology intersects with social psychology, and therefore this chapter is the most social-psychological one in the text. For those students who have already taken a course in social psychology, it might be useful to remind them of this fact and point out that the material in this chapter could seem familiar but will be interpreted rather differently than in most social psychology texts. Specifically, I treat lay personality judgments not merely as interesting perceptions but also as assessments that just might be accurate.

New in the Second Edition is a fuller treatment of the author's Realistic Accuracy Model of accuracy in personality judgment (see Figure 6.3 in the text).

TEACHING NOTES

It should not be difficult to convey the major point of this chapter, that personality assessment is a ubiquitous feature of daily life. Lectures can include numerous real-life examples, perhaps from the instructor's personal experience. It is also worth impressing on students the idea that the question of accuracy in personality judgment does not have a simple answer. It is not meaningful to say that people are generally accurate or inaccurate; instead we need to find out when people are more and less likely to be accurate. This is the purpose of the four moderators of accuracy discussed in this chapter (judge, target, trait, and information).

For instructors familiar with this background, the similarity between the model in Figures 6.2 and 6.3, and the Brunswik lens model could be developed in more detail. Research on the accuracy of personality judgment is active and the literature is rapidly expanding. An instructor might find it worthwhile to leaf through recent issues of the *Journal of Personality and Social Psychology, Journal of Personality,* and *Journal of Research in Personality* and look for articles by Colvin, Funder, Ickes, Kenny, Jussim, Paulhus, or Swann to bring the latest findings into the classroom.

PIECES OF THE PERSONALITY PUZZLE

Material on the accuracy of personality judgment—such as my own research—was not included in the reader for reasons of space and because it is often seen as being part of social psychology as well as or instead of personality psychology. An interested instructor could assign my theoretical article (*Psychological Review* 102 [1995]: 652–670). The O'Connor selection in Part II of the reader is a nice illustration of the everyday use of personality traits.

DISCUSSION QUESTIONS

1. When you judge the personality of others are you usually right or wrong?

2. When others judge your personality, are they usually right or wrong? When they are mistaken, why does this happen?

3. Under what circumstances do you find the personality of other people easiest to judge? Does your accuracy depend on the setting in which you meet them, what they are like, what you are like, or how you feel?

4. Under what circumstances do you find the personality of other people hardest to judge? Consider the same moderators as in question 3.

5. Have you taken a course in social psychology? If so, how was that course's treatment of the topic of person perception similar to and different from the present treatment of personality judgment?

MULTIPLE-CHOICE QUESTIONS

1. The judgments other people make of your personality may affect
   a. your opportunities.
   b. your chances of getting a job.

    c. your expectancies.

    d. all of the above.

Answer: d   Page: 115

Topic: Consequences of Lay Judgments of Personality

2. Self-fulfilling prophecies are more technically known as

    a. opportunistic fallacies.

    b. expectancy effects.

    c. consequential reputations.

    d. recency effects.

Answer: b   Page: 116

Topic: Consequences of Lay Judgments of Personality

3. Shy people fear social interactions and often feel lonely. They are typically perceived *by others* to be

    a. shy.

    b. cold and aloof.

    c. warm and friendly.

    d. sensitive and intelligent.

Answer: b   Page: 115

Topic: Consequences of Lay Judgments of Personality

4. Julie doesn't like to go to parties because she is afraid people won't like her. When she does go, she avoids eye contact, gives short abrupt responses to other people's questions, and quickly withdraws from all interactions. As a result, she spends most of the evening in a corner by herself, convinced that no one at the party likes her. This is an example of

    a. the causal force of I data.

    b. expectancy effects.

    c. the effects of low self-monitoring.

    d. an internal locus of control.

Answer: b   Page: 115

Topic: Consequences of Lay Judgments of Personality

5. In a series of studies about intellectual expectancies, Rosenthal and Jacobson (1968) found that the IQ of schoolchildren randomly identified as late bloomers increased by an average of about 15 points by the end of the school year. These studies demonstrated

    a. the power of expectancies.

    b. that formal training designed to develop self-efficacy can impact performance.

    c. the accuracy of lay judgments of personality.

    d. the good target moderator of accuracy.

Answer: a   Page: 116

Topic: Consequences of Lay Judgments of Personality

6. Research on intellectual and social expectancies demonstrates that
    a. other people's perceptions of your personality can influence who you are and what you do.
    b. other people's perceptions of your personality have little influence on your expectations.
    c. personality judgments are always based on direct observation of behavior.
    d. a and c.

Answer: a   Page: 118

Topic: Consequences of Lay Judgments of Personality

7. In a study of social expectancies, Snyder, Tanke, and Berscheid (1977) found that if a male subject had been shown a photograph of an attractive woman, the female subject
    a. rated herself as more attractive than the woman in the photograph.
    b. rated herself as less attractive than the woman in the photograph.
    c. was rated by other people as behaving in a warm, humorous, and friendly manner.
    d. was rated by other people as behaving in a cold, aloof, and unfriendly manner.

Answer: c   Page: 117

Topic: Consequences of Lay Judgments of Personality

8. Attractive females are expected to be warm and friendly, and those females who are considered to be attractive are treated in such a manner that they indeed respond in warm and friendly ways. According to Snyder, Tanke, and Berscheid (1977), this effect is a form of
    a. self-fulfilling prophecy.
    b. accuracy moderator.
    c. sex discrimination.
    d. the judgability phenomena.

Answer: a   Page: 117

Topic: Consequences of Lay Judgments of Personality

9. According to Lee Jussim (1991), the source of real-life expectancies is likely
    a. erroneous stereotypes about groups.
    b. previous observations of behavioral tendencies.

    c. authoritarian personality traits.

    d. a cognitive bias to seek incongruent information.

Answer: b   Pages: 118–119
Topic: Consequences of Lay Judgments of Personality

10. The complete assembly of all the judgments you make about your personality and all the opinions you have about yourself is called your

    a. self-monitor.

    b. sense of self-efficacy.

    c. self-concept.

    d. self-consciousness.

Answer: c   Page: 119
Topic: Consequences of Lay Judgments of Personality

11. Your perception of your own personality can affect

    a. your mood.

    b. your relationships.

    c. your behavior.

    d. all of the above.

Answer: d   Page: 120
Topic: Consequences of Lay Judgments of Personality

12. People who believe that the important forces within their lives come from within themselves and think that they can affect what happens to them

    a. have an external locus of control.

    b. have an internal locus of control.

    c. tend to be high self-monitors.

    d. tend to low self-monitors.

Answer: b   Page: 120
Topic: Consequences of Lay Judgments of Personality

13. Jeanine believes that no matter what she does, she won't have the wedding she's always dreamed about. Her mother will choose the bridal gown, caterer, and florist and she won't be able to do a thing about it. Jeanine most likely has

    a. high self-esteem.

    b. an internal locus of control.

    c. a tendency to self-monitor.

    d. an external locus of control.

Answer: d   Page: 120
Topic: Consequences of Lay Judgments of Personality

14. _____ refers to your beliefs about what you will and will not be able to accomplish.
    a. Self-efficacy
    b. Self-esteem
    c. Self-consciousness
    d. Self-generativity

    Answer: a   Page: 121
    Topic: Consequences of Lay Judgments of Personality

15. The basic that reason research on accuracy experienced a lengthy hiatus between 1955 and the mid-1980s was
    a. early researchers had already identified the characteristics of the good judge of personality.
    b. researchers turned their attention to studying the content of personality judgments.
    c. researchers lacked a consensual criteria for determining the accuracy of a personality judgment.
    d. early research indicated that personality judgments are relatively inconsequential.

    Answer: c   Page: 122
    Topic: The Accuracy of Lay Judgments of Personality

16. The statement "There is no such thing as objective reality, only human ideas or perceptions of reality" would most likely be made by a _____ The statement "The absence of perfect, infallible criteria for truth does not force us to conclude that all interpretations of reality are equally likely to be correct" would most likely be made by a _____.
    a. constructivist; social perceptualist
    b. constructivist; critical realist
    c. critical realist; social perceptualist
    d. a judgmentalist; critical realist

    Answer: b   Page: 122
    Topic: The Accuracy of Lay Judgments of Personality

17. The observation that if it looks like a duck, walks like a duck, and quacks like a duck, then it is probably a duck illustrates the method of
    a. moderator variables.
    b. constructivist accuracy.
    c. procedural judgment.
    d. convergent validation.

    Answer: d   Page: 123
    Topic: The Accuracy of Lay Judgments of Personality

18. Which of the following illustrates converging criteria that could be used to establish the accuracy of a personality judgment?
    a. One of your friends describes you as an extravert.
    b. You always show up to work on time and your colleagues say that you are dependable and conscientious.
    c. You tend to experience extreme emotions and throw tantrums frequently.
    d. You describe yourself as intelligent but you get a low score on an IQ test.

    Answer: b   Page: 123
    Topic: The Accuracy of Lay Judgments of Personality

19. One difficulty that early researchers encountered in identifying the good judge of personality was
    a. that a good judge in one context was not always a good judge in other contexts.
    b. that clinical psychologists dismissed the findings, claiming good judgment of others required extensive training.
    c. that the identified traits were not clearly a functional part of a specific ability to judge people.
    d. a and c.

    Answer: d   Pages: 123–124
    Topic: The Accuracy of Lay Judgments of Personality

20. Early research on the good judge of personality indicated that the good judge was
    a. extraverted.
    b. a high self-monitor.
    c. narcissistic.
    d. intelligent.

    Answer: d   Page: 124
    Topic: The Accuracy of Lay Judgments of Personality

21. Recent research by John and Robins (1994) indicates that _____ and _____ tend to be poor judges of personality.
    a. extraverts; depressives
    b. introverts; highly intelligent individuals
    c. narcissists; self-diminishers
    d. authoritarian personalities; high self-monitors

    Answer: c   Page: 124
    Topic: The Accuracy of Lay Judgments of Personality

22. In a study of the good judge of personality, Kolar, Funder, and Colvin (1996) used behavioral prediction as a criterion to compare the relative judgmental abilities of the self and acquaintances. Results indicated that
    a. the self judgments consistently had better predictive validity than the acquaintance judgments.
    b. acquaintance judgments consistently had better predictive validity than self judgments.
    c. there was no difference in the predictive validity of self and acquaintance judgments on any measures.
    d. the self judgments had better predictive validity but only for visible traits.

    Answer: b   Page: 124
    Topic: The Accuracy of Lay Judgments of Personality

23. Robert is a stable, well-adjusted person. His behavior is fairly consistent and predictable. Essentially, with Robert, "what you see is what you get." Robert would most likely be
    a. easy to judge accurately.
    b. a good judge of personality.
    c. a narcissist.
    d. a self-diminisher.

    Answer: a   Page: 126
    Topic: The Accuracy of Lay Judgments of Personality

24. According to research that shows a link between a trait's observability and the accuracy with which it is judged, which of the following traits would be easiest to judge accurately?
    a. Moodiness
    b. Talkativeness
    c. Ruminativeness
    d. All of the above

    Answer: b   Page: 127
    Topic: The Accuracy of Lay Judgments of Personality

25. Which of the following would moderate the ability to judge a specific trait?
    a. Judgability
    b. Unpredictability
    c. Visibility
    d. Acquaintanceship

    Answer: c   Page: 126
    Topic: The Accuracy of Lay Judgments of Personality

26. The finding that more-observable traits yield better interjudge agreement strongly suggests that peer judgment is based more on _____ than on _____.
    a. a manufactured reputation; the target's self judgments
    b. a manufactured reputation; direct behavioral observation
    c. direct behavioral observation; a manufactured reputation
    d. stereotypes; expectancies

    Answer: c   Page: 127
    Topic: The Accuracy of Lay Judgments of Personality

27. According to evolutionary theory, humans should be able to judge the trait of _____ more accurately than other traits that are less important for the survival of the species.
    a. social potency
    b. social closeness
    c. sociability
    d. sociosexuality

    Answer: d   Pages: 127–128
    Topic: The Accuracy of Lay Judgments of Personality

28. Dan's best friend Doug was his childhood friend and his college room-mate, and he has known him for over twenty years. Jim has only known Dan since he joined Jim's department at Acme Advertising Agency two months ago. According to Colvin and Funder's (1991) study of the boundaries on the acquaintanceship effect, if both Doug and Jim are asked to predict how Dan will behave during an ad presentation next week, whose predictions will be more accurate?
    a. Doug's.
    b. Jim's.
    c. The two predictions will be about equally accurate.
    d. Neither. Such behavior is not predictable.

    Answer: c   Page: 129
    Topic: The Accuracy of Lay Judgments of Personality

29. What was the boundary on the acquaintanceship effect identified by Colvin and Funder (1991)?
    a. The advantage of close acquaintances vanishes when the criterion is the ability to predict behavior in a situation similar to one that strangers have seen but that acquaintances have not.
    b. Judgments made by acquaintances who have known the target five years are equally as valid as judgments made by parents and acquaintances who have known the target twenty years.

c. Strangers' judgments are more accurate than acquaintances' judgments when the criterion is self-other agreement.

d. Strangers' judgments, based on five-minute videotaped observations of the target, demonstrated the ability to generalize to situations and contexts that were very different from the original videotaped interactions.

Answer: a   Page: 129
Topic: The Accuracy of Lay Judgments of Personality

30. Andersen (1984) found that the quality of information affected the accuracy of personality judgments. According to the results of this study, which kind of information would most likely lead to a social impression that corresponded to the target's self-assessment?
   a. Listening to the target describe his or her overt behavior
   b. Observing the person's behavior at work
   c. Watching a five-minute videotaped interaction between the target and an opposite-sex stranger
   d. Listening to the target describe his or her thoughts and feelings

Answer: d   Page: 131
Topic: The Accuracy of Lay Judgments of Personality

31. The Brunswikian lens model has been used to explain
   a. the process of construct validation.
   b. how to combine available environmental cues to make judgments.
   c. how an individual, through the lens of his or her own biased perceptions, constructs a personality trait in another person.
   d. why some traits are visible while others are not.

Answer: b   Page: 132
Topic: The Process of Accurate Judgment

32. A judge may see a target's behavior, pay attention to the behavior, and use the behavior in his or her judgment about the target's personality. However, for the personality judgment to be accurate, the
   a. observed behavior must be relevant to the trait being judged.
   b. behavior must be unusual and distinctive.
   c. judge must have observed the behavior on multiple occasions.
   d. personality trait must be cross-situationally consistent.

Answer: a   Page: 115
Topic: The Process of Accurate Judgment

33. I'm interested in knowing something about your personality, so I ask two of your friends about how sociable you are. Your two friends both say that you are very sociable. This is an example of

a. behavioral prediction.
b. accuracy.
c. interjudge agreement.
d. a and c.

Answer: c   Page: 123
Topic: The Accuracy of Lay Judgments of Personality

34. According to the Realistic Accuracy Model of personality judgment, the steps that occur when an accurate judgment of a personality trait is made are
a. validity → detection → convergence → accuracy.
b. personality → achievement → judgment → agreement.
c. detection → utilization → relevance → availability.
d. relevance → availability → detection → utilization.

Answer: d   Page: 134
Topic: The Process of Accurate Judgment

35. Imagine that you are at a party and your best friend introduces you to a guy named David. You and your friend talk to David for an hour, and you both notice the hostile comments that he repeatedly makes about his room-mate. Later, you and your friend discuss your impressions of David, and you find that you disagree about him. Your friend thinks that David's comments were just good-natured joking around and that he's a good guy and a pretty funny fellow. You think that his comments were mean spirited and that he's a hostile person. Your disagreement arises because you and your friend differ in the _____ stage of the RAM model of personality judgment.
a. detection
b. availability
c. utilization
d. judgment

Answer: c   Page: 134
Topic: The Process of Accurate Judgment

CHAPTER 7

Using Personality Traits to Understand Behavior

OUTLINE

SUMMARY

Traits are useful not just for predicting behavior but also for increasing our understanding of the basis of what people do. This chapter examined four basic approaches to the study of traits. The many-trait approach looks at the relationship between a particular behavior and as many different traits as possible. One technique used in this approach, the California Q-sort, assesses one hundred different traits at once. The Q-sort has been used to explore the basis of delay of gratification, drug use, depression, and political ideology. The single-trait approach zeros in on one particular trait deemed to be of special interest and its consequences for behavior; it has been used to study the traits of authoritarianism, conscientiousness, and self-monitoring, among other things. The essential-trait approach attempts to identify those few traits, out of the thousands of possibilities, that are central to understanding all of the others. The most widely accepted essential-trait approach is the Big Five, which lists as the essential traits to understand personality extraversion, neuroticism, conscientiousness, agreeableness, and openness. The typological approach attempts to capture the ways in which people might differ in kind, not just in degree. Recent research may have identified three basic types of personality: well-adjusted, maladjusted overcontrolled, and maladjusted undercontrolled.

ABOUT THE CHAPTER

Personality psychology's emphasis on the technology of assessment can sometimes lead to a misleading view of traits. They are often seen as dry, inert, uninteresting properties that lead to a lot of statistical manipulations but say little about human psychology. I think this a very mistaken view, and this chapter is an attempt to counter it with examples.

As I mentioned in the text, what makes personality assessment interesting is its usefulness for understanding behavior. In this chapter I show how traits can be used to understand delay of gratification, depression, and even Fascism, among other important phenomena. The point to emphasize is that the technology of personality assessment has opened windows to our understanding that otherwise would have remained closed.

This chapter plays a particularly important role in my self-appointed mission, described earlier, to sell psychology to students. The only way to show students that personality assessments teach us something worthwhile is by providing examples. That is the purpose of this chapter.

TEACHING NOTES

There is a lot of material in this chapter, but it is not particularly difficult. I will mention two potential stumbling blocks.

First, when considering what I call the many-trait approach, it is important to not let students get overwhelmed by tables such as Tables 7.2 through 7.5. Even psychologists sometimes get bogged down by paying too much attention to particular correlations or particular numbers. It is important, instead, to learn to look for general patterns that are consistent across all or nearly all the items in the table. I try to show how this is done in the text; an instructor could also help his or her students in this regard.

Second, the discussion of pseudoconservatism in the section on the authoritarian personality could stir some controversy. Pat Buchanan once wrote a newspaper column condemning work on the authoritarian personality (which apparently he never read) for demonizing the political right. Yet these authors were careful to distinguish genuine conservatism from radical, pseudoconservatism. This point may be worth emphasizing in lecture. Examples can often be taken from current events. The Republican nominee for President is usually a genuine conservative. Members of groups such as the Freemen, the Michigan Militia, or the Ku Klux Klan are pseudoconservatives.

PIECES OF THE PERSONALITY PUZZLE

Included in Part II of the reader are the original article on the Self-monitoring Scale (Snyder) and the latest exposition of the Big Five (by McCrae and Costa). The Self-monitoring article can be considered a classic. The Big Five article is particularly interesting for the way it tries to use the five traits to explain personality processes (a new development in this approach).

DISCUSSION QUESTIONS

1. From the examples in this chapter, which do you find yields the most insight— the many-trait, single-trait, or essential-trait approach?

2. Do you know people who abuse drugs? From your experience, what personality traits are associated with drug use? Are these traits a cause of drug abuse, a result of drug abuse, or both?

3. Do you know a male student who is depressed? A female student? Would you say their depression is of a different sort? How?

4. The concept of the authoritarian personality is half a century old. Is it still useful? Can you think of current examples besides those in the text?

5. If you could choose, would you rather be a high or low self-monitor?

6. Rate yourself or a good friend on the five essential traits of personality according to Costa and McCrae. Do you feel these ratings contain a lot of useful information? What essential aspects of personality do they leave out?

MULTIPLE-CHOICE QUESTIONS

1. From a scientific perspective, the central question about traits is
   a. how personality traits can be used to understand behavior.
   b. what are the important consequences of personality trait judgments.
   c. how personality traits combine to form our self-concept.
   d. whether different judges of the same person agree about the person's traits.

   Answer: a   Page: 138
   Topic: Using Personality Traits to Understand Behavior

2. A researcher taking the many-trait approach to understanding personality would likely use which of the following measurement instruments?
   a. California F Scale
   b. California Q-Set
   c. NEO Personality Inventory
   d. Self-monitoring Scale

   Answer: b   Page: 139
   Topic: The Many-Trait Approach

3. The _____ is a personality assessment device consisting of a deck of one hundred cards, each of which describes an aspect of personality. These cards are sorted into categories by the respondent.
   a. California F scale
   b. Self-monitoring Scale
   c. California Q-Set
   d. NEO Personality Inventory

   Answer: c   Page: 139
   Topic: The Many-Trait Approach

4. The most important advantage of Q-sorting is that it
   a. allows the judge to rate the target person consistently high or low on every trait.
   b. does not require the judge to make subtle discriminations between trait ratings.
   c. can only be used by trained clinicians, thus preventing problems inherent when laypersons serve as judges.
   d. forces the judge to compare all the items directly against each other.

   Answer: d   Page: 141
   Topic: The Many-Trait Approach

5. The items in the California Q-Set were derived from
   a. factor analysis.
   b. a formal empirical approach.
   c. Allport and Odbert's original list of trait terms from everyday language.
   d. efforts by clinicians to develop items that would describe their real cases.

   Answer: d   Page: 141
   Topic: The Many-Trait Approach

6. When reading a table of Q-sort correlates, the most important thing such tables show is
   a. the general patterns of correlates that emerge.
   b. the exact value of the correlations.
   c. the exact items that are present in the tables.
   d. b and c.

   Answer: a   Page: 142
   Topic: The Many-Trait Approach

7. According to the text, sex differences in delay of gratification are likely attributable to differences in
   a. hormones.
   b. attention span.
   c. socialization.
   d. temperaments.

   Answer: c   Page: 145
   Topic: The Many-Trait Approach

8. When a study uses rewards that are strongly desired and gives the subjects something to gain by waiting, then
   a. only ego resiliency will be related to delay.
   b. only intelligence will be related to delay.
   c. both intelligence and ego control will be related to delay.
   d. both ego resilience and submissiveness will be related to delay.

   Answer: c   Page: 145
   Topic: The Many-Trait Approach

9. Joe is a fifteen-year-old who abuses drugs on a regular basis. Research using the Q-sort suggests that, as a child, Joe would probably have been described as
   a. quiet and shy.
   b. overcontrolled and inhibited.

c. easily victimized and rigid.
d. emotionally unstable and aggressive.

Answer: d   Page: 143
Topic: The Many-Trait Approach

10. Jack Block found that twenty-three-year-olds who described themselves as being politically conservative were likely to have been described as _____ at age three.
   a. self-reliant and energetic
   b. easily victimized and rigid
   c. more likely to have developed close relationships
   d. emotionally unstable and aggressive

Answer: b   Page: 149
Topic: The Many-Trait Approach

11. Research on _____ addresses important questions concerning the relationship between inner reality and the private self, and external reality and the self as presented to others.
   a. authoritarianism
   b. introversion and extraversion
   c. self-monitoring
   d. conscientiousness

Answer: c   Page: 150
Topic: The Single-Trait Approach

12. Erich Fromm coined the term _____ to describe individuals who frequently turn their will over to a higher external authority but enjoy the experience of giving orders to those who are below them in the hierarchy.
   a. *authoritarian character*
   b. *politico-economic conservative*
   c. *fascist*
   d. *anti-intraceptive*

Answer: a   Page: 150
Topic: The Single-Trait Approach

13. Steve is extremely deferential to his boss. He complies immediately with all orders and never questions the decisions his boss makes. In his role as plant supervisor, Steve enjoys giving orders to the people he supervises and he gets very angry if they question those orders. Steve is probably
   a. a Republican.
   b. a low self-monitor.

c. an authoritarian personality.

d. a and c.

Answer: c   Pages: 150
Topic: The Single-Trait Approach

14. The California F-scale
   a. is the factor analytically derived scale designed to measure the Big Five personality factors.
   b. consists of one hundred trait descriptions that must be sorted into categories by judges.
   c. measures the psychological orientation that was believed to be the basis of racial prejudice and political conservatism.
   d. assesses the degree to which individuals repeatedly adjust their behavior across situations in order to behave appropriately and function effectively in each new situation.

Answer: c   Page: 151
Topic: The Single-Trait Approach

15. Adorno (1950) claimed that individuals who hold an internally consistent set of political beliefs that support institutions and the traditional social order while seeking to protect individual rights, property, and initiative are _____; those who show obvious contradictions between their acceptance of various conventional and traditional values and who tend to be cynical and punitive are _____.
   a. conservatives; liberals
   b. fascists; authoritarians
   c. liberals; conservatives
   d. conservatives; pseudoconservatives

Answer: d   Page: 156
Topic: The Single-Trait Approach

16. A frequent criticism of the authoritarian scale is that scores are affected by
   a. an acquiescence response set.
   b. a negativity bias.
   c. the judge's stereotypes.
   d. authoritarians' tendency to disagree with any statement.

Answer: a   Page: 158
Topic: The Single-Trait Approach

17. According to one survey, out of eighty-six possible employee qualities ranked by their importance by employers, seven out of the top eight qualities involved

a. intelligence.
b. agreeableness.
c. emotional stability.
d. conscientiousness.

Answer: d   Pages: 158–159
Topic: The Single-Trait Approach

18. In order to alleviate the effects of bias in employment testing, employers should use _____ because they typically do not show racial or ethnic differences or biases.
    a. aptitude tests
    b. ability tests
    c. tests of conscientiousness
    d. all of the above

    Answer: c   Pages: 159–160
    Topic: The Single-Trait Approach

19. The findings of Ones et al. (1993) suggest that the elusive motivation variable that distinguishes good workers from poor ones is
    a. self-monitoring.
    b. conscientiousness.
    c. emotional stability.
    d. ambition.

    Answer: b   Page: 160
    Topic: The Single-Trait Approach

20. Julie is a serious and conscientious employee; however, with her friends at Happy Hour on Friday afternoon she is the life of the party. According to Snyder's theory, Julie would most likely be
    a. a high self-monitor.
    b. a low self-monitor.
    c. high in private self-consciousness.
    d. low in public self-consciousness.

    Answer: a   Page: 161
    Topic: The Single-Trait Approach

21. Given Snyder's description of self-monitoring, you would expect someone who is a low self-monitor to be _____ than a high self-monitor.
    a. less judgable
    b. more judgable

c. more emotionally expressive

d. less behaviorally consistent

Answer: b   Page: 161

Topic: The Single-Trait Approach

22. Low self-monitors are more likely than high self-monitors to be described as
    a. talkative.
    b. self-dramatizing.
    c. having social poise and presence.
    d. independent.

Answer: d   Page: 163

Topic: The Single-Trait Approach

23. Henry Murray, the inventor of the TAT, theorized that twenty traits or
    needs were sufficient for understanding personality. Murray's approach
    to personality is similar to the
    a. empirical-trait approach.
    b. many-trait approach.
    c. essential-trait approach.
    d. hierarchical-trait approach.

Answer: c   Page: 166

Topic: The Essential Trait Approach

24. Which of the following approaches relies on factor analytic techniques to
    reduce the many traits in the English language down to few factors?
    a. Many-trait approach
    b. Single-trait approach
    c. Essential-trait approach
    d. Empirical-trait approach

Answer: c   Page: 166

Topic: The Essential-Trait Approach

25. Which of the following reflect the structure of personality presently
    proposed by many adherents of the essential-trait approach?
    a. Neuroticism, extraversion, openness, agreeableness, and conscientiousness
    b. Authoritarianism, fascism, conservatism, anti-Semitism, and cynicism
    c. Traits of the California Q-Set
    d. Self-monitoring

Answer: a   Page: 166

Topic: The Essential-Trait Approach

26. The lower your score is on measures of happiness, well-being, and health, the
    a. higher your score is on agreeableness.
    b. higher your score is on neuroticism.
    c. higher your score is on self-monitoring.
    d. lower your score is on authoritarianism.

    Answer: b   Page: 167
    Topic: The Essential-Trait Approach

27. An objection to the Big Five is
    a. that the factors are correlated with one another.
    b. that it is not clear that the Big Five are five entirely separate and independent traits.
    c. that a good deal of information about personality cannot be reduced to those five traits.
    d. all of the above.

    Answer: d   Page: 167
    Topic: The Essential-Trait Approach

28. Cross-cultural research on the Big Five suggests that
    a. the same Big Five are found in all cultures that have been studied to date.
    b. none of the factors appear to replicate cross-culturally.
    c. the central attributes of personality are generally similar in other cultures but there are important differences cross-culturally.
    d. some of the U.S. factors are found in studies using European samples but none of the U.S. factors are found in studies with Asian samples.

    Answer: c   Page: 169
    Topic: The Essential-Trait Approach

29. Authoritarian people are _____ to people with a higher rank or status than their own but are _____ to people of a lower rank or status
    a. submissive and respectful; disrespectful and contemptuous
    b. disrespectful and contemptuous; submissive and respectful
    c. conscientious and neurotic; agreeable and extraverted
    d. distrustful and irritable; talkative and socially poised

    Answer: a   Page: 152
    Topic: The Single-Trait Approach

30. People who adjust their behavior to fit the situation are called _____, and people whose behavior is guided by their personality are called _____.
    a. ego resilient; ego controlled
    b. neurotic; conscientious
    c. high self-monitors; low self-monitors
    d. low self-monitors; high self-monitors

    Answer: c   Page: 161
    Topic: The Single-Trait Approach

31. The _____ approach to personality usually assumes that all people can be characterized by points on a continuous score of measurement; the _____ approach to personality suggests that people might differ in kind more than in degree.
    a. typological; trait
    b. trait; typological
    c. essential-trait; single-trait
    d. constructivist; critical realist

    Answer: b   Page: 169
    Topic: Typological Approaches to Personality

32. In a review of the research on personality typologies, Caspi (1998) identified three basic types of people. Which of the following was *not* one of these personality types?
    a. Well-adjusted person
    b. Maladjusted extraverted person
    c. Maladjusted undercontrolling person
    d. Maladjusted overcontrolling person

    Answer: b   Page: 171
    Topic: Typological Approaches to Personality

CHAPTER 8

Anatomy, Biochemistry, and
Personality

OUTLINE

B. Biology, Cause, and Effect

VI. Summary

SUMMARY

Brain anatomy and neurophysiology are both relevant to personality. Observations of animals suggest that the human brain resembles three brains in one: a reptilian, a paleomammalian, and a neomammalian brain. This structure suggests that humans and animals have many basic brain functions in common, but also it is important to remember that all species are adapted for unique environments and have evolved unique brain structures. What we know about brain functioning in humans comes from the observation of people who have suffered accidental brain damage or undergone brain surgery. Damage to the frontal lobes, for example, seems to affect planning, foresight, and emotional regulation. Examinations of individuals who have suffered such damage suggest that emotions and judgment are surprisingly closely connected. The amygdala is important for emotions, and the two cerebral hemispheres seem to have different functions: the right hemisphere is more intuitive and the left hemisphere is more analytic; the right hemisphere seems to specialize in negative emotions and the left hemisphere in positive emotions. For a time, surgery was used on the frontal lobes and other areas of the brain in an attempt to affect behavior, but this did not turn out to be a worthwhile approach. Theories by Hans Eysenck and Jeffrey Gray describe postulated brain mechanisms, such as arousal or inhibitory systems, that affect major dimensions of personality, such as extraversion and anxiety. Both theories suggest that brain underarousal can lead to a syndrome that includes sensation-seeking, dangerous, and even criminal behavior, and a good deal of subsequent research has borne out this suggestion.

Research on the physiology of personality has explored the effects of neurotransmitters such as norepinephrine, dopamine, and serotonin. Other research has examined the effects of hormones—primarily the male sex hormone testosterone and the stress hormone cortisol—on personality. The relationship between anatomy, physiology, and personality is complex, but an integrative model by Zuckerman provides a start toward organizing and understanding them by describing the interactions between five levels of psychological and biological functioning. Finally, it is important to remember that biological processes affects behavior, but behavior and the social environment both affect biological processes. An understanding of each will be helpful for understanding the other.

ABOUT THE CHAPTER

Research in the biology of personality is exceedingly complex and expanding at a rapid rate. Moreover, it is not yet well integrated, either with the study of personality or within itself. The biological study of personality includes four separate subfields, each of which is biological but has relatively little in common with the others. These are the study of brain anatomy, of the physiology of the nervous system, of behavioral genetics, and of evolutionary biology. These four approaches fall into two groups; the first two topics are considered in Chapter 8, and the second two in Chapter 9. But it is worth keeping in mind, and conveying to students, that these are better described as four biological approaches rather than four facets of a biological approach.

Much of what passes for research on the anatomy and physiology of personality is about 85 percent biology and 15 percent personality, if that. Very often, complex physiological measures are compared to simplistic indicators of personality such as questionable self-report questionnaires. But some solid findings are beginning to emerge, and this chapter is a survey of some of the more clear and important ones.

The chapter includes a brief review of the anatomy of the nervous system and the physiology of synaptic transmission. Some students will have been exposed to this material before, either in introductory psychology or in biological psychology courses. The material included here is what I judged to be the bare minimum for understanding the rest of the discussion. An instructor with particular interest and expertise in this area could easily supplement my discussion of anatomy and physiology with further illustration and detail.

This area of research is developing rapidly and several new studies are included in the Second Edition. There is also some new case study information, including new details about Phineas Gage (and a pair of remarkable photographs of his skull), a case of frontal lobe damage called Elliott, and the case of Charles Whitman (the Texas Tower sniper, who had a brain tumor). Damasio's somatic marker hypothesis is also included in the Second Edition.

The chapter tries to attain a balance between an appreciation for the work that has been done in this area, and an avoidance of presenting the results as if the biology of personality is on the verge of being completely understood. It isn't. The biological study of personality is still in its very early stages. Much has been accomplished, much remains to be done, the field is complex, and further progress will require increasingly hard work, and perhaps a bit more attention to psychological issues along with biological ones.

TEACHING NOTES

As mentioned above, the chapter presents a bare minimum of detail about the anatomy and physiology of the nervous system. I did not want to duplicate material better handled in a general course on biological psychology. But for an interested instructor, it should be easy to present more detail than included here. Damasio's book on Descartes's error is a useful source.

The relationship between neurochemicals, drugs, and personality opens up interesting avenues for lecture and discussion. An interested instructor might pick up Kramer's book *Listening to Prozac* and develop a presentation of Kramer's idea of cosmetic psychopharmacology, and its pros and cons.

The integrative model by Zuckerman (Figure 8.10) will strike most students as frightening. They certainly should not be expected to memorize it, or even understand it in any detail. I included it in the book to illustrate the different levels of analysis in the study of the biological basis of personality and to show how complex an analysis is required to even begin to show how the different levels are interrelated. A student who grasps that much has grasped the essentials and should be reassured on that point.

A final observation is that in early drafts of the First Edition I included this biological material within the trait section! Notice how many studies in this chapter (and the next) stem directly from the trait approach. On the one hand, a trait is measured (e.g., aggressiveness). On the other hand, a physiological parameter is assessed (e.g., testosterone level). Then the two are correlated. The close connection between the biological and trait approach is not always recognized, so may be worth pointing out to students.

PIECES OF THE PERSONALITY PUZZLE

The historical selection by Wells in Part III of the reader presents an old humoural theory of personality of the Galen variety. The Dabbs et al. piece on testosterone and Blum's review article are up-to-date examples of current findings in the biological study of personality, directly relevant to this chapter.

DISCUSSION QUESTIONS

1. What do you think of Eysenck's account of extraversion and introversion? Think of the people you know. Is somebody who would rather stay at home with a book than go to a wild party avoiding overstimulation? Is the party goer ordinarily understimulated?

2. What if Charles Whitman had survived that awful day in Texas? Would it have been fair to prosecute him for murder?

3. Psychosurgery has mostly given way to drug therapy. Is this an improvement? Does it make any difference whether a person's behavior or mood is controlled with drugs than with surgery?

4. If you could take a pill to improve some aspect of your personality, would you do it? Would you still be same person after taking the pill?

5. Let's say you are in intense negotiations with somebody. Your adversary takes a pill to make himself or herself more confident and aggressive, and thereby achieves a better outcome than you do. Did your adversary have an unfair advantage?

MULTIPLE-CHOICE QUESTIONS

1. The _____ forms the core of the human brain and is the basic structure around which the rest of the organ is built.
    a. neomammalian brain
    b. paleomammalian brain
    c. reptilian brain
    d. hippocampus

    Answer: c   Page: 182
    Topic: The Anatomy and Function of the Brain

2. The reptilian brain includes the
    a. limbic system, hypothalamus, and amygdala.
    b. cerebral cortex, corpus callosum, and association cortex.
    c. occipital lobe, parietal lobe, and temporal lobe.
    d. thalamus, amygdala, and cerebellum.

    Answer: d   Page: 182
    Topic: The Anatomy and Function of the Brain

3. The thick outer layer of tissue that is the seat of cognitive activities such as language, planning, and self-awareness is the
    a. cerebellum.
    b. cerebral cortex.
    c. amygdala.
    d. hypothalamus.

    Answer: b   Page: 184
    Topic: The Anatomy and Function of the Brain

4. The case of railroad worker Phineas Gage illustrated that
    a. brain injuries will affect physical but not psychological functioning.
    b. injuries to the brain can affect personality and behavior.
    c. the amygdala has important effects on fear and anger.
    d. the right hemisphere is the province of image-oriented, intuitive thinking.

    Answer: b   Pages: 188–189
    Topic: The Anatomy and Function of the Brain

5. Reports about the remarkable behavioral and personality effects of accidental brain injury in the frontal lobe led
    a. researchers to search for additional psychotropic drugs to treat mental disorders.

b. to an increased understanding of the role of the cerebral cortex in emotional regulation.

c. neurosurgeons to perform lobotomies to control maladaptive behavior.

d. to all of the above.

Answer: c   Page: 191
Topic: The Anatomy and Function of the Brain

6. Some psychologists have suggested that personality traits such as chronic anxiety, fearfulness, sociability, and sexuality have a physical basis in the
   a. frontal lobe.
   b. amygdala.
   c. ventromedial cortex.
   d. left hemisphere.

Answer: b   Pages: 193–194
Topic: The Anatomy and Function of the Brain

7. In 1966, Charles Whitman killed his wife, his mother, and fourteen more people at the University of Texas before he was killed by police. To discover if a physical disorder could have been responsible for this rampage of violent motivations and emotions, an autopsy was performed and revealed a tumor in Whitman's
   a. frontal lobe
   b. amygdala
   c. ventromedial cortex
   d. left hemisphere

Answer: b   Page: 194
Topic: The Anatomy and Function of the Brain

8. The right hemisphere of the brain is primarily responsible for _____ while the left hemisphere controls _____.
   a. rational thought; intuitive thought
   b. verbal skills; analytic thinking
   c. emotional regulation; rational thought
   d. schizophrenia; mood disorders

Answer: c   Page: 195
Topic: The Anatomy and Function of the Brain

9. People who have suffered damage to the right hemisphere of their brain have manifested
   a. schizophrenia.
   b. obsessive disorders.

c. multiple personality disorder.

d. manic-depressive psychoses.

Answer: d   Page: 195

Topic: The Anatomy and Function of the Brain

10. According to Eysenck, differences between introverts and extraverts are attributable to the functioning of the

a. limbic system.

b. ARAS.

c. hormones.

d. frontal cortex.

Answer: b   Page: 196

Topic: The Anatomy and Function of the Brain

11. According to Eysenck, introverts are _____ while extraverts are _____.

a. overaroused by the ARAS; underaroused by the ARAS

b. underaroused by the ARAS; underaroused by the limbic system

c. overaroused by the limbic system; underaroused by the limbic system

d. unaffected by testosterone; unaffected by estrogen

Answer: a   Page: 196

Topic: The Anatomy and Function of the Brain

12. Ricardo likes to drive fast cars, and enjoys bungee jumping and going to noisy nightclubs. According to Eysenck's theory, it is likely that Ricardo is _____ whose ARAS causes him to be chronically _____.

a. a neurotic; overstimulated

b. a neurotic; understimulated

c. an extravert; overaroused

d. an extravert; underaroused

Answer: d   Page: 196

Topic: The Anatomy and Function of the Brain

13. Eysenck linked differences between neurotics and emotionally stable individuals to the functioning of

a. the limbic system.

b. the ARAS.

c. hormones.

d. the frontal cortex.

Answer: a   Page: 197

Topic: The Anatomy and Function of the Brain

14. According to Eysenck's theory, which type of person should exhibit greater salivation in the lemon juice test?
   a. An extravert
   b. An introvert
   c. A neurotic
   d. A stable person

   Answer: b   Page: 198
   Topic: The Anatomy and Function of the Brain

15. According to Gray's theory, there are two basic systems underlying person-ality. The _____ system causes a person to be sensitive to rewards and motivated to attain them, and the _____ system causes a person to be sensitive to punishments and motivated to avoid them.
   a. reward; punishment
   b. approach; inhibition
   c. fight; flight
   d. ARAS; limbic

   Answer: b   Page: 200
   Topic: The Anatomy and Function of the Brain

16. Zuckerman has recently integrated a synthesis of current knowledge about brain functions with the concepts proposed by
   a. Galen.
   b. Costa and McCrae
   c. Eysenck and Gray.
   d. Darwin.

   Answer: c   Page: 201
   Topic: The Anatomy and Function of the Brain

17. Galen suggested that there were _____ basic types of personality linked to excess amounts of _____.
   a. five; hormones
   b. three; neurotransmitters
   c. four; bodily humors
   d. two; inhibitory neural mechanisms

   Answer: c   Page: 203
   Topic: The Biochemistry of Personality

18. According to Galen, an excess of yellow bile would cause a person to be
   a. depressed and melancholy.
   b. cold and apathetic.

c. cheerful and robust.

d. angry and bitter.

Answer: d   Page: 203
Topic: The Biochemistry of Personality

19. According to research by modern health psychologists, the choleric, or chronically hostile, person seems to be at risk for
a. heart attack.
b. cancer.
c. stroke.
d. all of the above.

Answer: a   Page: 203
Topic: The Biochemistry of Personality

20. Chemicals that either facilitate or inhibit communication from one nerve cell to another are called
a. synapses.
b. hormones.
c. neurotransmitters.
d. inhibitory communicators.

Answer: c   Page: 205
Topic: The Biochemistry of Personality

21. People with chronically high levels of norepinephrine tend to
a. be anxiety-prone and dependent.
b. be susceptible to Parkinson's disease.
c. exhibit hypomanic excitement and restlessness.
d. suffer from clinical depression.

Answer: a   Page: 207
Topic: The Biochemistry of Personality

22. Wayne tends to suffer from chronic pessimism, is hypersensitive to rejection, worries obsessively, and is prone to sudden bursts of irrational anger. Wayne is exhibiting the symptoms of
a. high norepinephrine levels.
b. serotonin depletion.
c. hormonal imbalance.
d. low dopamine levels.

Answer: b   Page: 208
Topic: The Biochemistry of Personality

23. One criticism of the widespread use of the drug Prozac is that it
    a. is currently prescribed only for norepinephrine depletion.
    b. does not appear to affect personality at all.
    c. likely causes serotonin depletion.
    d. does not produce predictable effects on personality.

    Answer: d   Page: 209
    Topic: The Biochemistry of Personality

24. The biological chemicals that are released from the gonads, the hypothalamus, and the adrenal cortex are called
    a. synapses.
    b. hormones.
    c. neurotransmitters.
    d. inhibitory communicators.

    Answer: b   Page: 210
    Topic: The Biochemistry of Personality

25. Aggressive behavior has been linked to
    a. a failure in dopamine reuptake.
    b. synaptic decay.
    c. high testosterone levels.
    d. an estrogen imbalance.

    Answer: c   Page: 211
    Topic: The Biochemistry of Personality

26. In one study, male U.S. military veterans were asked about their past behaviors. Those with higher testoterone levels more often reported
    a. having assaulted others.
    b. having very few sexual partners.
    c. problems with depression.
    d. experiencing delusions.

    Answer: a   Page: 211
    Topic: The Biochemistry of Personality

27. Men with high levels of testosterone
    a. are always more aggressive than men with low levels of testosterone.
    b. are not necessarily aggressive.
    c. are extremely likely to commit aggravated rape.
    d. tend to have more education and are wealthier than men with low levels of testosterone.

    Answer: b   Pages: 211–213
    Topic: The Biochemistry of Personality

28. The relationship between testosterone and physical aggression holds only or most strongly for
    a. relatively uneducated men from low economic classes.
    b. very educated men from high economic classes.
    c. relatively uneducated women and both educated and uneducated men.
    d. all men regardless of education or class background.

    Answer: a   Page: 211
    Topic: The Biochemistry of Personality

29. One problem researchers experience when attempting to directly link testosterone to aggression and sexuality is
    a. that the relationships have never been studied in women.
    b. that testosterone seems to affect sexual desire in men but not in women.
    c. that it is difficult to determine the causal direction since aggression and sex can affect testosterone levels.
    d. b and c.

    Answer: c   Page: 213
    Topic: The Biochemistry of Personality

30. Which hormone is sometimes called the flight or fight hormone?
    a. Testosterone
    b. Estrogen
    c. Progesterone
    d. Cortisol

    Answer: d   Page: 213
    Topic: The Biochemistry of Personality

31. Maria tends to be an impulsive sensation seeker who is disinclined to follow societal rules and norms. Even very dangerous activities do not seem to elicit much of a fear response from her. It is likely that Maria has abnormally
    a. high levels of testosterone.
    b. low levels of testosterone.
    c. high levels of cortisol.
    d. low levels of cortisol.

    Answer: d   Page: 214
    Topic: The Biochemistry of Personality

32. In Zuckerman's hierarchical model of the biological basis of personality, _____ lie at the fifth and lowest level of analysis.
    a. supertraits
    b. emotions

c. neurotransmitters
d. reward expectations

Answer: c   Page: 215
Topic: The Biochemistry of Personality

33. To learn more about the relationship between personality and brain structures, psychologists have studied
a. people who have suffered accidental brain damage.
b. people who have had brain surgery.
c. the metabolic activity of living human brains.
d. all of the above.

Answer: d   Page: 187
Topic: The Anatomy and Function of the Brain

34. Before brain surgery, Elliot was a good husband and father and held a responsible job. After removal of a brain tumor below the ventromedial cortex (in the frontal lobe of the brain), Elliot's personality changed in what way?
a. He began to experience visual hallucinations.
b. He began to experience auditory hallucinations.
c. His emotional reactions and decision making abilities were impaired.
d. a and b.

Answer: c   Page: 190
Topic: The Anatomy and Function of the Brain

35. According to Damasio's somatic marker hypothesis, damage to the ventromedial cortex impairs one's _____; this then impairs one's _____.
a. emotional reactions to events and thoughts; ability to make decisions about what is and is not important
b. primary visual and auditory cortexes; ability to distinguish real sensory stimulation from hallucinations
c. reptilian brain; ability to perform creative activities as opposed to fixed action patterns
d. none of the above; none of the above

Answer: a   Page: 190
Topic: The Anatomy and Function of the Brain

CHAPTER 9

The Inheritance of Personality: Behavioral Genetics and Evolutionary Theory

OUTLINE

SUMMARY

Behavioral genetics and evolutionary biology both concern how personality might be inherited from one's parents and ancestors. Behavioral genetics addresses individual differences in behavioral traits and examines how parents transmit traits to their children and how biological relatives tend to be psychologically similar. Many personality traits are heritable in this sense, but this finding does not mean that personality is solely determined by genetics. The environment remains critically important. Evolutionary biology explains patterns of behavior that are characteristic of the entire species, such as aggression, altruism, and mating, as being those that have been useful for reproductive success as the human species evolved. Some of these explanations are controversial. But research on evolutionary biology and behavioral genetics does imply that biology and genetic inheritance are involved in the determination of human personality. Biology will never take over the functions of other areas of personality research and theory. As exemplified by Bem's theory of the development of sexual orientation, the promise of the biological approaches comes from their potential to illuminate the interactions between biological, personality, social, and sociological influences on behavior.

ABOUT THE CHAPTER

This chapter covers two very different ways of considering the biological inheritance of personality. The first, behavioral genetics, focuses exclusively on individual differences. Like the trait approach, its research design captures differences between people rather than aspects of personality all people have in common. Indeed, nearly all studies in behavioral genetics are based on assessments of the similarities among relatives according to self-report personality questionnaires.

The chapter presents the basic tool of research on behavioral genetics, the heritability coefficient. This statistic is explained because it is ubiquitous in research on behavioral genetics and even appears frequently in the popular media. But its usage is confusing. Behavioral geneticists all acknowledge that the heritability coefficient is *not* a nature-nurture ratio that quantifies the relative importance of genes versus environment. But the number is often discussed as if that were exactly what it meant, so the chapter cautions against this misinterpretation. This leaves us with this question: What *does* a heritability coefficient mean? In my opinion, just this: When the heritability of a given trait is greater than 0, which it nearly always is, then the trait is affected by genetic factors in some way.

New to the Second Edition is the discussion of Harris's claim that the family is not important for psychological development, a claim based largely on the behavioral genetic finding concerning the low importance of the shared family environment. It does not appear that this claim is destined to be taken seriously for very long (if it still is), but it does open a wide door toward interesting discussions and arguments about the psychological importance of the family.

The other biological approach in this chapter addresses human nature rather than individual differences. The evolutionary biology of personality seems to assume that all people—or at least all people of each gender—are basically the same, and the question is how evolution shaped people to be this way. This approach is controversial, especially when it touches on topics such as sex differences in mating strategies. Psychologists are divided as to the political implications of this work, and the quality of the reasoning that links theory to data. Clearly an evolutionary explanation of a behavioral pattern cannot be directly proven, but research can poke at issues around the edges. Some examples, such as the infidelity scenario studies, are included in the chapter.

The discussion of the evolutionary approach has been updated in the Second edition. In particular, the critique and response section has been revised. The discussion of the teleological fallacy has been omitted, and a consideration of the Eagly-Wood critique has been added.

An important issue alluded to in this and the preceding chapter is that of biological reductionism. Some biologically oriented psychologists seem to believe that in the end, all of psychology—even personality psychology—will reduce to biology. The chapter includes a section arguing against this point of view, basically on the ground that biological and psychological analyses address fundamentally different issues. It concludes with a summary of Daryl Bem's theory of sexual orientation and presents it as an example of the kind of analysis that is needed to bring biological and psychological issues closer to each other. Perhaps in the future we will see more analyses like this, of other important psychological phenomena.

TEACHING NOTES

It would be useful for the instructor to emphasize the difference between a study of personality that focuses on individual differences as opposed to one that focuses on human nature. Behavioral genetics and evolutionary biology provide good examples of the two emphases.

The material on the heritability coefficient might be difficult to teach. The exact psychological interpretation of this statistic is still a matter of debate, and it is commonly used in the literature in ways I do not think can be justified. Depending on an instructor's interest and expertise, one might wish either to skip over much of this material in class and simply note the area is controversial, or go into greater detail about exactly how heritabilities are calculated and what they mean. New studies reporting heritabilities appear in the newspapers all the time; an instructor who watches for these can bring this current material to class and perhaps spark a discussion of what it means.

A related complication arises with respect to the big news from behavioral genetics, that the shared family environment has little or no influence on personality development. This is an important claim that needs to be taught to students.

But it might be premature to teach it as a matter of settled fact. For one thing, the finding is based on data almost entirely limited to self-report questionnaires. Aspects of personality not captured by such questionnaires are not (yet) included in this general conclusion. Another complication is that many years of research in developmental psychology has documented the effects of family size, poverty, and parental mental illness on personality development. These are all aspects of the shared family environment, and the conclusions of this vast literature have not yet been integrated with the recent conclusions of research on behavioral genetics. A third complication is that research appearing since the First Edition has begun to question the conclusion both on methodological grounds (e.g., analyses of the effects of restricted range of families in adoption studies) and empirical grounds (e.g., findings that aggressiveness and behavioral tendencies measured through observation rather than self-report show shared family effects). This newer literature is included, briefly, in the Second Edition.

Students with a feminist orientation sometimes find the evolutionary explanations of sex differences offensive. I would recommend that they be encouraged to work through just what they find to be wrong about this approach and articulate their objections as clearly as possible. This could be the basis of a useful and memorable class discussion that—regardless of what the class concludes about sex differences—could result in a solid understanding of basic evolutionary principles.

For different reasons, some students might find the presentation of Bem's theory of sexual orientation to be problematical. But this is a good time to demonstrate, by example, that psychological research and analysis can provide a useful way of looking at topics—such as homosexuality—that so often trigger little more than heated opinions. The Bem theory is included in this chapter as an example—the only example to date, I know of—of an analysis that combines biological and environmental determinants of behavior in a truly integrative manner. The main point I hope students carry away is not any particular view of homosexuality but a conception of how sophisticated analysis can connect genetic, hormonal, environmental, and societal variables to explain an important psychological outcome.

PIECES OF THE PERSONALITY PUZZLE

From Part III of the reader, articles by Bouchard and by Plomin present state of the art expositions of behavioral genetics from two of the most important researchers in the field. The selection on the evolutionary biology of jealousy, by Buss et al., is summarized in this chapter. The paper by Wilson and Daly is one of the more inflammatory pieces I have seen concerning the evolution of sex differences. The Eagly and Wilson article is perhaps the most cogent critique of the evolutionary approach to personality to be published thus far. Finally, Bem's article presenting his theory of the developmental of sexual orientation is included in the reader.

DISCUSSION QUESTIONS

1. What is human nature? If your goal is to understand human nature, what topics must you address?

2. Do you think your own personality was shaped more by how you were raised or by the genes you were born with?

3. If you have siblings, do you think the family environment in which you grew up was the same or different from that of your siblings? If different, do you think these differences account for how you and your siblings turned out differently?

4. Do you agree or disagree with evolutionary biology's conclusions about sex differences? Do you think these differences exist in the way they are described? Do you find it plausible that they could have an evolutionary explanation? Or do you think they are explained as well or better by culture? Why? (*Note*: If a student argues that culture explains these differences, the class could be asked to explain where culture comes from!)

5. Do you think psychology will ever be reduced to biology?

6. (Caution with this one) Do you agree with Bem's explanation of the development of sexual orientation? In particular, do you think exotic becomes erotic? Can you think of examples other than those Bem describes?

MULTIPLE-CHOICE QUESTIONS

1. The approach that attempts to explain how individual differences in behavior (i.e., personality traits) are passed from parent to child and thus are shared by biological relatives is called
   a. evolutionary biology.
   b. behavioral genetics.
   c. heritability science.
   d. behavioral Darwinism.

   Answer: b   Page: 218
   Topic: The Inheritance of Personality

2. The approach that attempts to explain how patterns of behavior that are characteristic of the entire human species had their origins in the survival value they had for our ancestors is called
   a. evolutionary biology.
   b. behavioral genetics.

c. heritability science.
d. behavioral Darwinism.

Answer: a   Page: 218
Topic: The Inheritance of Personality

3. Monozygotic twins share _____ of the genes that vary across
individuals and dizogotic twins share, on average, _____ of the
genes that vary across individuals.
a. 50 percent; 25 percent
b. 90 percent; 10 percent
c. 50 percent; 100 percent
d. 100 percent; 50 percent

Answer: d   Page: 219
Topic: Behavioral Genetics

4. Behavioral genetics, like trait psychology, focuses exclusively on the inheritance of traits that _____ while evolutionary biology focuses on
the inheritance of traits that _____.
a. all humans share; differ from one individual to another
b. vary among groups of individuals; vary among individuals
c. differ from one individual to another; all humans share
d. are species-specific; are individual-specific

Answer: c   Page: 219
Topic: Behavioral Genetics

5. The basic assumption of behavioral genetics is that if a trait is influenced by
genes, then it ought to be more highly correlated across pairs of _____
than across pairs of _____.
a. genetic siblings; fraternal twins
b. fraternal twins; identical twins
c. identical twins; fraternal twins
d. adoptive siblings; genetic siblings

Answer: c   Page: 219
Topic: Behavioral Genetics

6. If the correlation between the shyness of a sample of dizygotic twin pairs
is .25 and the correlation between the shyness of a sample of monozygotic
twin pairs is .50, then the heritability coefficient for shyness is:
a. .25.
b. .75.

    c. .125.

    d. .50.

Answer: d   Page: 220

Topic: Behavioral Genetics

7. The incidence of schizophrenia was measured in both MZ and DZ twins. The correlation between MZ twins was .50 and the correlation between the DZ twins was .30. What is the heritability coefficient for schizophrenia?

    a. .80

    b. .20

    c. .40

    d. .65

Answer: c   Page: 220

Topic: Behavioral Genetics

8. According to estimates based on twin studies, the average heritability of many traits of personality is about

    a. .10.

    b. .20.

    c. .40.

    d. .60.

Answer: c   Page: 220

Topic: Behavioral Genetics

9. Estimates of heritability obtained in studies using nontwin samples indicate that the heritability of personality traits is about

    a. .10.

    b. .20.

    c. .40.

    d. .60.

Answer: b   Page: 221

Topic: Behavioral Genetics

10. According to some experts, a large heritability index for a specific personality trait can legitimately tell us

    a. that nature matters more than nurture for that trait.

    b. that shared family environment exerts a large influence on that personality trait.

    c. that genes matter for that personality trait.

    d. all of the above.

Answer: c   Page: 221

Topic: Behavioral Genetics

11. If there is no variation in a trait, then the heritability of that trait will be approximately
    a. 1.00.
    b. .50.
    c. .25.
    d. .00.

    Answer: d   Page: 225
    Topic: Behavioral Genetics

12. Recent theorizing maintains that traits with high heritabilities are likely to be those traits that
    a. are very important for survival or reproductive fitness.
    b. have not been important for survival or reproductive fitness.
    c. have no variation across individuals.
    d. b and c.

    Answer: b   Pages: 225–226
    Topic: Behavioral Genetics

13. Which of the following is *not* a limitation of the heritability coefficient?
    a. It does not tell you whether specific behavioral or mental disorders are part of the normal range or are pathologically distinctive.
    b. It does not yield a conceptual understanding of how personality develops.
    c. It does not indicate the degree to which a trait is determined by genes as opposed to the environment.
    d. None of the above.

    Answer: a   Pages: 224–226
    Topic: Behavioral Genetics

14. Isaac inherited a tendency toward sensation seeking. As a result, he likes to experiment with various dangerous drugs and has become involved with the drug culture. He has recently begun to rob liquor stores with his new friends. Isaac's experiences illustrate
    a. that the inherited trait of sensation seeking caused him to become a criminal.
    b. that the environment is what creates criminal behavior.
    c. that there is a link between inherited traits and the environment the person seeks out because of that trait.
    d. none of the above.

    Answer: c   Page: 229
    Topic: Behavioral Genetics

15. Timothy, as a result of his genes, went through puberty later than his peers. Because he was much smaller than other boys, they tended to pick on him, and he fought back to protect himself. As a young adult, Timothy is much more aggressive than most of his peers. The effects on Timothy's personality (i.e., he is aggressive) are
    a. completely the result of his genetic inheritance.
    b. completely the result of his early social environment.
    c. the result of an interaction between the genetic expression and the resulting social environment.
    d. the result of his social environment in adulthood since genes cannot affect behavior in adulthood.

    Answer: c   Page: 229
    Topic: Behavioral Genetics

16. According to evolutionary biology, altruistic behavior might help assure the survival of one's own genes into succeeding generations primarily because
    a. if the people who share your genes survive, then some of your genes will make it into the next generation.
    b. altruistic people tend to attract more mates, thereby increasing the likelihood that altruistic people will reproduce.
    c. altruistic individuals take fewer risks than nonaltruistic individuals, so they are more likely to survive and produce children.
    d. all of the above.

    Answer: a   Page: 231
    Topic: Evolutionary Theory

17. Across a wide variety of cultures, _____ are more likely than _____ to place a higher value on physical attractiveness.
    a. women; men
    b. introverts; extraverts
    c. extraverts; introverts
    d. men; women

    Answer: d   Page: 232
    Topic: Evolutionary Theory

18. When placing personal ads women are more likely to specify that the person they are seeking be _____, while men are more likely to specify that the person they are seeking be _____.
    a. younger than they; older than they
    b. the same age as they; younger than they

c. older than they; younger than they
d. older than they; the same age as they

Answer: c   Page: 232
Topic: Evolutionary Theory

19. Kara is placing a personal ad in the local paper. According to evolutionary research on mate selection, Kara will probably emphasize her _____ when describing herself.
a. physical attractiveness
b. future goals
c. financial resources
d. personality traits

Answer: a   Page: 232
Topic: Evolutionary Theory

20. Kevin is placing a personal ad in the local paper. According to evolutionary research on mate selection, Kevin will probably emphasize his _____ when describing himself.
a. physical attractiveness
b. future goals
c. financial resources
d. personality traits

Answer: c   Page: 232
Topic: Evolutionary Theory

21. The evolutionary explanation of sex differences in mate selection is that
a. men and women are seeking very different things. Men are just seeking sex and women are seeking commitment.
b. the differences are the result of a biological fluke and will disappear completely in the next hundred years.
c. men and women are seeking essentially the same thing. Both are trying to increase the likelihood they will produce viable offspring who will survive.
d. the differences are the result of socialization practices.

Answer: c   Page: 232
Topic: Evolutionary Theory

22. According to evolutionary theory, the reason men tend to be very concerned about their partner's sexual infidelity is that they are concerned
a. that their partner will leave them for another person.
b. that they are not the biological father of the children they are supporting.

c. that their partner will form an emotional bond with another person.
d. a and c.

Answer: b   Page: 234
Topic: Evolutionary Theory

23. According to evolutionary theory, women tend to be very concerned about their partner's emotional infidelity because they are concerned
   a. that their partner will leave them for another person.
   b. that their partner will share resources that belong to them and their children with another woman and her children.
   c. that their partner will form an emotional bond with another person.
   d. all of the above.

Answer: d   Page: 234
Topic: Evolutionary Theory

24. The idea that some women follow a different reproductive strategy than most of their sisters is called
   a. the sexy son hypothesis.
   b. taking the reproductive high road.
   c. the adaptive option proposal.
   d. evolutionary roaming.

Answer: a   Pages: 234–235
Topic: Evolutionary Theory

25. Which of the following is an objection to evolutionary theory?
   a. Evolutionary theorizing consists of after-the-fact speculations that can't be put to empirical test.
   b. Evolutionary theorists assume that you do not have to be consciously aware of your wish to reproduce for it to determine your behavior.
   c. Evolutionary theorists assume that those behavior patterns that are present today are essentially inevitable and unchangeable because they are rooted in our biology.
   d. All of the above.

Answer: d   Pages: 235–236
Topic: Evolutionary Theory

26. The idea that once everything is known about brain structure and physiology, we will be able to reduce everything about the mind to biology is called
   a. the teleological fallacy.
   b. biological reductionism.

c. psychophysical structuralism.

d. physiological fundamentalism.

Answer: b   Page: 240

Topic: Will Biology Replace Psychology?

27. Bem's theory of sexual orientation maintains that
    a. homosexuality is purely the result of biological variables.
    b. sexual orientation is the primarily the result of early socialization practices.
    c. the same basic processes underlie homosexuality and heterosexuality.
    d. we tend to seek out and be attracted to others who are very familiar to us.

Answer: c   Page: 241

Topic: Putting It All Together: Sexual Orientation

28. An important aspect of Bem's theory of sexual orientation is that it
    a. shows what a biologically informed theory of personality should look like.
    b. proves what causes sexual orientation in humans.
    c. illustrates the interaction of many different kinds of elements to produce sexual orientation.
    d. a and c.

Answer: d   Page: 243

Topic: Putting It All Together: Sexual Orientation

29. What finding from research in behavioral genetics would support the idea that shared family environment has little effect on personality development?
    a. The personality traits of MZ twins are correlated at .50 on average.
    b. The personality traits of DZ twins are correlated at .30 on average.
    c. The personality traits of adoptive siblings raised in the same family are correlated only at .05.
    d. The personality traits of adoptive siblings raised in the same family are correlated above .25.

Answer: c   Page: 222

Topic: Behavioral Genetics

30. Drawing on research addressing the impact of the shared family environment on personality development, Harris argued
    a. that parents have no important long-term effects on their children's personality.
    b. that parents have important long-term effects on their children's personality.

c. that parents' behavior affects the personality of their genetic offspring more than their adopted children.

d. none of the above.

Answer: a   Page: 223
Topic: Behavioral Genetics

31. A response to the conclusions drawn from behavioral genetics research on the shared family environment is that
    a. some behavioral genetics research shows that shared family environment matters.
    b. research shows that environmental factors such as social class and styles of child rearing do affect personality development.
    c. perhaps the personality measures that are typically used in studies of behavioral genetics researchers do not adequately capture the essence of personality as it emerges from family experience.
    d. all of the above.

Answer: d   Pages: 223–224
Topic: Behavioral Genetics

32. Offering an alternative, nonevolutionary view of gender differences in mate selection, Eagly and Wood (1999) suggest
    a. that societies norms reflect men's greater size and strength and women's role in childbearing more than biologically wired behavioral tendencies.
    b. that societies norms reflect biologically wired behavioral tendencies more than men's greater size and strength and women's role in childbearing.
    c. that mate selection norms emerge from different levels of norepinepherine that the sexes have.
    d. none of the above.

Answer: a   Page: 238
Topic: Evolutionary Theory

33. The world is changing toward more industrialization, in which physical strength matters less and alternative child-care arrangements are possible. The view that men and women's behavioral tendencies are determined by social structure implies that
    a. men's and women's behavioral tendencies will change over thousands of years, if at all
    b. men's and women's behavioral tendencies will change relatively quickly (over hundreds of years).
    c. men's and women's behavioral tendencies will probably never change.
    d. men will primarily adopt child-rearing duties and women will primarily adopt duties of rulers and warriors.

Answer: b   Page: 238
Topic: Evolutionary Theory

CHAPTER 10 | Basics of Psychoanalysis

SUMMARY

Unlike many other approaches to personality, the psychoanalytic approach concentrates on the cases where the cause of behavior is mysterious and hidden.

Psychoanalytic theory is complex, but it is based on a relatively small number of key ideas, including psychic determinism, internal structure, mental energy, and psychic conflict. Throughout its history psychoanalysis has been controversial, although the nature of the controversy has changed with the times. Freud himself was one of the geniuses of the twentieth century.

Freud's psychoanalytic theory posits two fundamental motives, a life drive, or libido, and a drive toward death and destruction. Libido produces psychic energy, and the story of psychological development is the story of how this energy is focused in different areas at four different stages of life. The main issue for the oral stage is dependency; for the anal stage it is obedience and self-control; for the phallic stage it is gender identity and sexuality; and for the genital stage it is maturity, in which ideally one learns to balance love and work and to be productive in both domains. Fixation occurs when an individual gets stuck in one of these stages into adulthood; regression is a movement backward from a later psychological stage to an earlier one.

Freud's theory divides the mind into three parts: the id, ego, and superego. These parts correspond roughly to emotions, cognition, and conscience, respectively. Primary process thinking is a primitive style of unconscious thought, characterized by association, displacement, symbolization, and an irrational, uncompromising drive toward immediate gratification. Secondary process thinking is ordinary rational, conscious thought. There are three layers to consciousness: the conscious mind, the preconscious, and the unconscious. The essence of psychoanalytic therapy, performed through techniques such as dream analysis and free association in the context of a therapeutic alliance between patient and therapist, is to bring the unconcious thoughts that are the source of an individual's problems into the open, where the conscious, rational mind can deal with them.

ABOUT THE CHAPTER

This chapter combines and to some degree condenses material included in two chapters in the First Edition. It begins with an overview of the impact and basic philosophy of psychoanalysis and moves on to include a presentation of the basic drives, the stages of development, fixation, regression, and the tripartite theory of mind and consciousness, as well as a brief discussion of psychotherapy.

The presentation is *not* orthodox Freud or anything like it, and I do not draw close connections between actual statements by Freud and what is said in this chapter. Many other books are available that do that. Rather, my intention is to present the basic ideas and outlook of psychoanalytic thought in a modern context, and in as persuasive a way as I can manage. This chapter and the next try to sell Freud to students.

Freud died more than half a century ago, and because he changed his theory often during his lifetime, it seems likely he would have continued to do so had he lived another sixty years. Perhaps his new version would have looked like the one in these chapters; we will never know, of course. In any case, rather than provide a literal rendering of Freud's views, I have presented an interpretation based on those aspects of his theory that, after all these years, I find still persuasive.

The reader will find very little about the Oedipal crisis or penis envy, both important parts of the theory to Freud. I don't find those accounts persuasive, so I deemphasize them in favor of the parts of the theory I do find persuasive. Other changes in emphasis, similar in kind but relatively minor, will also be found in these chapters.

TEACHING NOTES

When I first began teaching the introductory personality course, I was surprised to learn that the section on psychoanalysis was—for me, at least—the easiest to teach. It takes a real struggle to bring some parts of personality psychology to life for the student. Freud is easy.

Sometimes psychoanalysis is taught with a close attention to theoretical detail and disputes among the major psychoanalytic theorists. It is obvious that this is not my approach. An instructor might wish to emphasize to students that the material in their text is an interpretation rather than literal rendition of Freudian psychoanalytic thought. An interesting class discussion might be developed around the question of whether this is a good way to teach Freud.

For an introductory course, I recommend that an instructor emphasize examples from daily life that illustrate psychoanalytic issues (such as the Associated Press story that begins the section; new ones like this appear constantly). An instructor who wishes to go beyond this text might want to present some of Freud's famous cases, which I barely mention. A good source for such cases is the Freud reader that Peter Gay edited (see "Recommended Readings" in the text). These cases could be used to bring Freud's theorizing to life or, depending on the instructor's inclination, to show how psychoanalytic reasoning ventures far from the data and goes fundamentally astray.

An instructor who wishes to present the "real" Freud might present lectures based directly on Freud's writings, and some of the controversies he involved himself in. A survey of Freud's major works is missing from these chapters; an instructor might want to include that in lecture. Finally, I say relatively little about Freud's theory of relation between the individual and society, as espoused in *Civilization and its Discontents*; this could make an excellent topic for a lecture or two.

If the students in the course include any English majors, they might be asked how psychoanalysis is used in the analysis of literature. Later in the text, I will also claim that most athletic coaches are Freudian. This fact could also be extracted from a class discussion if there are athletes in the room. Finally, after all these years, arguments about Freud still appear regularly in both the professional literature and popular media. Be on the lookout.

A final note considering the coverage of psychoanalysis. Many psychologists—especially but not only those outside the subfield of personality—have a low opinion of Freud and of psychoanalysis, and sometimes make contemptuous, mocking remarks about both. It is probably already obvious that I will not do this. I have a great respect for Freud and his theory, find it truly insightful, and present the best case for it that I can. An instructor with a strong antipathy to Freud will want to present the opposing side, and the dynamics of such a disagreement between text and instructor could, if properly handled, be highly stimulating and educational for students.

PIECES OF THE PERSONALITY PUZZLE

The reader includes two excerpts from Freud's original writings and I would assign them both.

DISCUSSION QUESTIONS

1. Do you hear Freudian ideas used in the way people talk about each other? Can you think of any examples beyond those given in the text?

2. Has anything happened recently in the news or in your daily life that seems best explained from a psychoanalytic perspective?

3. Have you heard Freud or psychoanalytic ideas used in any other courses you have taken, in or out of the psychology department?

4. When instructors of your other courses have mentioned Freud, have they expressed a basically favorable or hostile attitude? On what grounds?

5. What do you think it means about a theorist for people to still be arguing heatedly about his ideas almost a century later?

6. Do you think toilet training is a big deal for children? Does the way it is handled have important consequences for how they develop into adults?

7. Research in political science shows that most young adults belong to the same political party as their parents. How would Freud explain this? What do you think is the reason?

8. Can you think of any oral, anal, phallic, or genital characters among the people you know? Without naming names, what are they like? How do you think they got this way?

9. Do you think dreams reveal anything important about the mind of the dreamer? Have you ever learned something about yourself by analyzing a dream you had?

10. If you had a personal, psychological problem, would you go to a psychoanalyst? Why or why not?

MULTIPLE-CHOICE QUESTIONS

1. The assumption that everything that happens in a person's mind and everything a person does has a specific cause that can be identified is called the assumption of
   a. psychic determinism.
   b. mental causality.
   c. psychological determination.
   d. libidinal functionalism.

   Answer: a   Page: 253
   Topic: Psychic Determinism

2. The deterministic explanation for the behavior of the prostitute-patronizing city prosecutor, described in the text, would be
   a. that the explanation for the prosecutor's behavior lies in the dynamics of his personality.
   b. that the prosecutor decided to get a prostitute of his own free will.
   c. that the prosecutor's behavior is inconsistent and difficult to predict.
   d. b and c.
   e. a and b.

   Answer: a   Page: 253
   Topic: Psychic Determinism

3. Jason is playing with his brother's new skateboard. He runs it into a wall and breaks it to pieces. Psychoanalysts would maintain that the destruction of the skateboard was
   a. just an accident.
   b. probably determined by some unconscious desire in Jason to ruin his brother's new toy.
   c. a conscious free choice made by Jason right before he ran it into the wall.
   d. caused by the environmental conditions.

   Answer: b   Page: 254
   Topic: Psychic Determinism

4. Unlike other perspectives, the psychoanalytic perspective emphasizes the importance of _____ in determining behavior.
   a. conscious desires
   b. environmental influences

   c. self-efficacy

   d. unconscious processes

Answer: d   Page: 259

Topic: Psychic Determinism

5. According to Freud, the internal structure of the mind consists of

   a. the oral, anal, and phallic stages.

   b. the id, ego, and superego.

   c. libido and Thanatos.

   d. psychic energy and psychic conflict.

Answer: b   Page: 254

Topic: Internal Structure

6. According to Freud, the irrational and emotional part of the mind is the
_____ and the rational part of the mind is the _____.

   a. superego; ego

   b. id; libido

   c. libido; Thanatos

   d. id; ego

Answer: d   Page: 254

Topic: Internal Structure

7. According to Freud, the mental energy that makes the mind function
is called

   a. the id.

   b. Thanatos.

   c. the libido.

   d. sublimation.

Answer: c   Page: 255

Topic: Mental Energy

8. Jenny spends a lot of her psychic energy trying to repress or push out of
consciousness her memory of a recent mugging. According to Freud, if
Jenny is trying to write a novel, she will find

   a. that the repression has created additional psychic energy and that will
make her more creative.

   b. that she has little psychic energy left to spend on her writing.

   c. that she will be able to easily shift the energy from the memory
repression to the novel writing.

   d. none of the above.

Answer: b   Page: 255

Topic: Mental Energy

9. According to the text, the prosecutor's psychic conflict about patronizing a prostitute likely resulted in the
   a. ego's winning out over the superego.
   b. superego's winning out over the id.
   c. id's winning out over the superego.
   d. ego's winning out over the id.

Answer: c   Page: 255
Topic: Psychic Conflict

10. Tracy has a big test tomorrow. Rationally, she knows she should study for it tonight, but she really wants to go to Gregg's party and enjoy herself. When she considers not studying and going to the party instead, her conscience bothers her and she feels guilty. She decides to stay home and study for the test so she doesn't feel guilty. According to psychoanalytic theory, Tracy's
    a. ego won out over her superego.
    b. superego won out over her id.
    c. id won out over her superego.
    d. ego won out over her id.

Answer: b   Pages: 255, 277
Topic: Psychic Conflict

11. The criticism of Freud's ideas that is most popular today, particularly among academics, is that _____. The criticism of Freud's ideas that was most prevalent at the time that it was first introduced was that _____.
    a. Freud placed too much emphasis on sex and sexual energy; Freud relied too heavily on controlled, systematic studies
    b. Freud's theory is unscientific; Freud placed too much emphasis on sex and sexual energy
    c. Freud relied too heavily on controlled, systematic studies; Freud placed too much emphasis on sex and sexual energy
    d. Freud maintains that behavior is largely the result of rational thought processes; Freud's theory is unscientific

Answer: b   Page: 256
Topic: The Controversial Nature of Psychoanalysis

12. The therapeutic technique that involves instructing the patient to say whatever comes to mind is called
    a. free association.
    b. systematic regression.
    c. repressed memory recovery.
    d. reaction formation.

Answer: a   Page: 258
Topic: Freud Himself

13. Freud called the fundamental force that was necessary for creation, protection, and enjoyment of life _____. The idea that the basic tendency of ordered systems is toward disorder and chaos is similar to Freud's concept of _____.
    a. Thanatos; libido
    b. libido; Thanatos
    c. the primary process; the secondary process
    d. fixation; regression

    Answer: c   Page: 259
    Topic: Psychoanalysis, Life, and Death

14. Allen has just broken up with his long-time girlfriend Katy. According to the doctrine of opposites, how will Allen respond to the breakup?
    a. He will regress to an earlier stage of development.
    b. He will switch from being an oral character to being an anal character.
    c. He will try to find a woman who is a little bit different from Katy.
    d. He will begin to despise Katy.

    Answer: d   Page: 261
    Topic: Life and Death

15. The _____ is the idea that psychic energy can neither be created nor destroyed.
    a. doctrine of opposites
    b. conservation principle
    c. energy fixation corollary
    d. theory of internal resource management

    Answer: b   Page: 261
    Topic: Life and Death

16. According to Freud, the process of psychological development is driven by the
    a. investment and redirection of psychic energy.
    b. development of key psychosocial relationships with others.
    c. development of autonomy.
    d. conflict between the conscious and preconscious mind.

    Answer: a   Page: 262
    Topic: Psychological Development

17. The main psychological theme of the oral stage of development is
    a. jealousy.
    b. morality.

c. control.

d. dependency.

Answer: d   Page: 263

Topic: Oral Stage

18. Baby Jessica's parents respond to her every need as soon as she cries. Freud would predict that, as an adult, Jessica will

a. be well adjusted.

b. be passive.

c. rebel against authority figures.

d. become sexually promiscuous.

Answer: b   Page: 264

Topic: Oral Stage

19. During the anal stage, parents insist that the child _____. Following from this, an anal character is consistently dealing with issues of

_____.

a. remain passive and dependent; dependency and passivity

b. relinquish his or her attachment to the opposite-sex parent; jealousy and sexual identity

c. exhibit self-control and obedience; control and authority relations

d. be assertive and productive; creation and enhancement of life

Answer: c   Pages: 266–267

Topic: Anal Stage

20. Two-year-old Jonathan knows he is not allowed to have a second piece of candy. When his mother is distracted, he takes another piece out of the candy jar just to see if he can get away with it. Jonathan is in the _____ stage of development.

a. phallic

b. oral

c. anal

d. latency

Answer: c   Page: 267

Topic: Anal Stage

21. Stephen's apartment is exceptionally neat and clean while Mary Anne's house is always messy. According to Freud,

a. Stephen is an anal character and Mary Anne is an oral character.

b. Stephen is an oral character and Mary Anne has regressed to the latency period.

   c. both have developed fixations in the phallic stage.

   d. both are anal character types.

Answer: d   Page: 268
Topic: Anal Stage

22. According to Freud, the physical focus of the phallic stage is the
   a. penis for boys and the vagina for girls.
   b. anus for boys and the mouth for girls.
   c. penis for both boys and girls.
   d. womb for boys and the penis for girls.

Answer: c   Page: 269
Topic: Phallic Stage

23. The basic developmental task of the phallic stage is
   a. the acquisition of gender identity.
   b. the development of self-control.
   c. forming relationships with an opposite-sex peer.
   d. accomplishing learning tasks such as reading and writing.

Answer: a   Page: 270
Topic: Phallic Stage

24. According to Freud, boys and girls figure out what it means to be male and female
   a. by being rewarded or punished for gender-appropriate behavior.
   b. through the process of identification.
   c. during the genital stage of development.
   d. all of the above.

Answer: b   Page: 270
Topic: Phallic Stage

25. In the last two years, Marcus has had over three dozen sexual partners. Marcus has likely developed a fixation in the
   a. genital stage.
   b. oral stage.
   c. latency period.
   d. phallic stage.

Answer: d   Page: 270
Topic: Phallic Stage

26. The genital character type
   a. tends to be sexually promiscuous.
   b. is dependent on other people.

c. is psychologically well adjusted.

d. operates according to the pleasure principle.

Answer: c   Page: 271

Topic: Genital Stage

27. Joe developed a fixation in the phallic stage. When he experiences a great deal of stress at work, Joe will likely become

a. disorganized.

b. uninterested in sex.

c. dependent and passive.

d. overcontrolled and anxious.

Answer: b   Page: 273

Topic: Moving through Stages

28. Leaving a disproportionate amount of libido behind at a childhood stage of development is called

a. regression.

b. fixation.

c. transference.

d. the secondary process.

Answer: b   Page: 273

Topic: Moving through Stages

29. When she is scared, twenty-five-year-old Maria becomes very passive and dependent. Maria is experiencing

a. regression.

b. transference.

c. sublimation.

d. libidinal restructuring.

Answer: a   Page: 273

Topic: Moving through Stages

30. The _____ brain primarily deals with basic emotions and motivation and is analogous to the _____.

a. neomammalian; superego

b. paleomammalian; id

c. reptilian; id

d. paleomammalian; ego

Answer: c   Pages: 273–274

Topic: The Id

31. Modern ego psychologists believe that the key function of the ego is to
    a. form compromises between the different parts of the mind.
    b. make sense of personal experiences.
    c. seek pleasure.
    d. a and b.

    Answer: d   Page: 275
    Topic: The Ego

32. The superego maintains its power through its ability to create
    a. dreams.
    b. anxiety.
    c. psychic energy.
    d. fixations.

    Answer: b   Page: 277
    Topic: The Superego

33. Unconscious thought is generally due to _____ and conscious thought is generally due to _____.
    a. primary process thinking; secondary process thinking
    b. regression; repression
    c. secondary process thinking; primary process thinking
    d. superego functioning; id functioning

    Answer: a   Page: 277
    Topic: Primary and Secondary Process Thinking

34. According to Freud, symbols in dreams
    a. are the result of primary process thinking.
    b. are a way for unconscious thoughts to become conscious.
    c. have meanings that vary for every individual.
    d. all of the above.

    Answer: d   Page: 278
    Topic: Primary and Secondary Process Thinking

35. The largest and most important level of consciousness in Freud's topographic model of the mind is the
    a. conscious mind.
    b. ego.
    c. unconscious mind.
    d. id.

    Answer: c   Page: 279
    Topic: Consciousness

36. The primary goal of psychoanalytic therapy is to
    a. bring unconscious conflicts into conscious awareness.
    b. teach the client to repress id impulses.
    c. regress the client to earlier levels of functioning through hypnosis.
    d. have the therapist become emotionally involved with the client.

    Answer: a   Page: 280
    Topic: Psychoanalytic Therapy

CHAPTER 11 | Defenses and Slips

SUMMARY

Anxiety can have its origins in the real world or in inner, psychic conflict, such as that produced by an impulse of the id that the ego and superego try to combat. The ego has several defense mechanisms to protect against the conscious experience of excessive anxiety and its associated negative emotions, such as shame and guilt. These defense mechanisms include denial, repression, reaction formation, projection, rationalization, intellectualization, displacement, and sublimation. Forbidden impulses of the id can occasionally be expressed in thought and behavior in two ways. Parapraxes are accidental ventings of forbidden impulses in the kind of accidents of speech or action commonly called Freudian slips. In wit, a forbidden impulse is deeply disguised in such a way as to permit its enjoyment without anxiety. A joke is not funny when this disguise is insufficient.

ABOUT THE CHAPTER

Most of the comments about Chapter 10 also apply to Chapter 11. I would suggest that they be assigned together.

New in the Second Edition is that some of Baumeister et al.'s summary of research on the defense mechanisms is integrated into the text.

TEACHING NOTES

Students find lectures on the defense mechanisms particularly interesting. It is easy and fun to generate numerous examples; students can be encouraged to come up with their own. It is also a good use of class time to develop more examples of slips and their interpretation and to tell some jokes and try to psychoanalyze them according to the theory presented in this chapter.

PIECES OF THE PERSONALITY PUZZLE

Baumeister's summary of empirical research relevant to the defense mechanisms is directly relevant to the material in this chapter.

DISCUSSION QUESTIONS

1. Do you think you can be anxious about something without knowing what it is? Or does that strike you as a nonsensical idea?

2. What examples of the various defense mechanisms—in your own behavior or that of others—can you come up with?

3. Athletes in the class: Is your coach a Freudian?

4. What's the funniest joke you have heard lately? Can you explain, from a psychoanalytic perspective, what makes it funny? Have you heard a joke lately that you did not find funny? Can you explain what went wrong?

MULTIPLE CHOICE QUESTIONS

1. The primary result of psychic conflict is
   a. depression.
   b. aggression.
   c. anxiety.
   d. immorality.

   Answer: c   Page: 284
   Topic: Anxiety

2. Diana, a married woman, is contemplating having an affair with an attractive man in her department. How would Diana's ego likely respond?
   a. It would encourage her to pursue the affair immediately.
   b. It would object to the affair because it seems immoral.
   c. It would object to the affair because it seems impractical.
   d. It would make Diana feel guilty.

   Answer: c   Page: 284
   Topic: Sources of Anxiety

3. Trisha, who is on a diet, passes by a bakery and sees a chocolate cake in the window. She immediately wants to go in and get the cake, but then realizes that eating the cake will only destroy her diet and feels guilty for even thinking about breaking her diet. Trisha is experiencing
   a. psychic conflict.
   b. delay of gratification.
   c. sublimation.
   d. reaction formation.

   Answer: a   Page: 284
   Topic: Sources of Anxiety

4. Which part of the personality is responsible for creating defense mechanisms?
   a. Unconscious mind
   b. Ego
   c. Superego
   d. Conscious mind

   Answer: b   Pages: 283, 286
   Topic: Defense Mechanisms

5. Strategies that help individuals cope with anxiety, guilt, and shame are called
   a. compensatory processes.
   b. regressive tendencies.

    c. fixations.

    d. defense mechanisms.

Answer: d   Page: 286
Topic: Defense Mechanisms

6. Zeke has just found out that his brother was killed in a plane crash. His first response is "No, not John; he's not dead." According to psychoanalytic theory, Zeke is experiencing the operation of

    a. a parapraxis.

    b. a fixation.

    c. a defense mechanism.

    d. an id impulse.

Answer: c   Page: 287
Topic: Defense Mechanisms—Denial

7. Brian and Matt have both just flunked out of college. Brian is sure he didn't flunk and that he really is going to graduate. Matt simply refuses to think about what just happened. Brian is using the defense mechanism of _____ and Matt is using _____.

    a. denial; intellectualization

    b. rationalization; repression

    c. reaction formation; rationalization

    d. denial; repression

Answer: d   Pages: 287–290
Topic: Defense Mechanisms—Denial and Repression

8. Ruth is a biology major who hates her current biology class. Which of the following would be an example of Ruth repressing her feelings about the class?

    a. Forgetting to bring home the homework for the class

    b. Accidentally oversleeping and missing the class

    c. Neglecting to call her lab partner

    d. All of the above

Answer: d   Pages: 288–290
Topic: Defense Mechanisms—Repression

9. Angie has completely repressed any memory of the sexual abuse she experienced as a child. Lately, she has been experiencing extreme stress at work and is going through a traumatic divorce. Angie will probably

    a. begin to recall the sexual abuse.

    b. experience a failure of her defense mechanism.

c. experience anxiety.
d. all of the above.

Answer: d   Pages: 288–290
Topic: Defense Mechanisms—Repression

10. The defense mechanism of _____ keeps forbidden thoughts, feelings, and impulses out of awareness by replacing them with their opposites.
a. parapraxis
b. projection
c. reaction formation
d. displacement

Answer: c   Page: 290
Topic: Defense Mechanisms—Reaction Formation

11. One explanation of extreme homophobia is that it is the result of
a. reaction formation.
b. displacement.
c. denial.
d. rationalization.

Answer: a   Page: 290
Topic: Defense Mechanisms—Reaction Formation

12. _____ involves attributing your unwanted impulses and feelings to another person.
a. Displacement
b. Projection
c. Repression
d. Compensation

Answer: b   Page: 292
Topic: Defense Mechanisms—Projection

13. Debbie accuses her husband of having an affair because she is secretly attracted to the next-door neighbor. Debbie is likely _____ her own feelings.
a. projecting
b. repressing
c. rationalizing
d. displacing

Answer: a   Page: 292
Topic: Defense Mechanisms—Projection

14. According to the text, the most frequently used defense mechanism is probably
    a. repression.
    b. denial.
    c. reaction formation.
    d. rationalization.

    Answer: d   Page: 293
    Topic: Defense Mechanisms—Rationalization

15. Mark claims that it is okay for him to take supplies from his employer because he uses some of them to do office work at home. Mark is using the defense mechanism of
    a. repression.
    b. denial.
    c. rationalization.
    d. intellectualization.

    Answer: c   Pages: 293–294
    Topic: Defense Mechanisms—Rationalization

16. If you deal with an unpleasant or threatening feeling by turning it into a thought, you are using
    a. rationalization.
    b. intellectualization.
    c. repression.
    d. reaction formation.

    Answer: b   Page: 294
    Topic: Defense Mechanisms—Intellectualization

17. Chris spends most of the time before his surgery calmly discussing the death rates associated with the illness and the surgery with his doctor, reading all the latest medical articles on the disease, and studying all the surgical procedures. He views his illness as an interesting opportunity to learn more about medicine. Freud would say that Chris was using _____ to deal with his illness.
    a. denial
    b. rationalization
    c. repression
    d. intellectualization

    Answer: d   Page: 294
    Topic: Defense Mechanisms—Intellectualization

18. Dennis is very attracted to his boss Heidi. Instead of asking her out, he asks his neighbor Karen to go out with him. Dennis is _____ his feelings for his boss.
    a. displacing
    b. projecting
    c. denying
    d. rationalizing

    Answer: a   Page: 295
    Topic: Defense Mechanisms—Displacement

19. The defense mechanism of _____ involves relocating the object of an emotional response or desire from an unsafe target to a safe one.
    a. projection
    b. displacement
    c. transference
    d. transmutation

    Answer: b   Pages: 295–296
    Topic: Defense Mechanisms—Displacement

20. Experimental research evidence indicates that a person who displaces aggression will
    a. be less inclined to be aggressive in general.
    b. be more inclined to be aggressive in general.
    c. use rationalization as a defense mechanism.
    d. use projection as a defense mechanism.

    Answer: b   Page: 296
    Topic: Defense Mechanisms—Displacement

21. The works of Leonardo da Vinci and Michelangelo were, according to Freud, examples of
    a. fixation.
    b. intellectualization.
    c. sublimation.
    d. projection.

    Answer: c   Page: 297
    Topic: Defense Mechanisms—Sublimation

22. If a woman pursued an acting career because she craved attention and adulation, Freud would probably say she
    a. was regressing to the anal stage of development.

b. was sublimating her forbidden impulses.

c. had developed a fixation during the phallic stage.

d. had an unresolved Electra complex.

Answer: b   Page: 297
Topic: Defense Mechanisms—Sublimation

23. _____ are the result of unsuccessful attempts by the ego and superego to control forbidden impulses.
   a. Parapraxes
   b. Fixations
   c. Defense mechanisms
   d. Repressed memories

Answer: a   Page: 298
Topic: The Expression of Impulse—Parapraxes

24. A parapraxis is another name for a
   a. slip of the tongue.
   b. fixation.
   c. repressed memory.
   d. sublimation.

Answer: a   Page: 298
Topic: The Expression of Impulse—Parapraxes

25. Dan was in a hurry and forgot to kiss his wife good-bye before leaving for work. Freud would say that
   a. the stress of being late made Dan forget.
   b. Dan's behavior is a symptom of fixation in the genital stage.
   c. Dan may be harboring some form of hostility toward his wife.
   d. forgetting the kiss was an accident.

Answer: c   Page: 298
Topic: The Expression of Impulse—Parapraxes

26. If you commit a slip of the tongue when you are tired, Freud would say
   a. that the slip was an accident.
   b. that the slip was caused by the fatigue.
   c. that fatigue made it easier for the impulse to be expressed.
   d. a and b.

Answer: c   Page: 300
Topic: The Expression of Impulse—Parapraxes

27. Controlled expressions of forbidden impulses are the basis of _____ while uncontrolled expressions are the basis of _____.
    a. forgetting; slips of the tongue
    b. wit; parapraxes
    c. bad jokes; funny jokes
    d. projection; displacement

    Answer: b   Page: 301
    Topic: The Expression of Impulse—Wit

28. In a successful joke, the forbidden impulse is
    a. disguised.
    b. repressed.
    c. obvious.
    d. expressed directly.

    Answer: a   Page: 303
    Topic: The Expression of Impulse—Wit

29. When a person uses the defense mechanism of denial, he or she _____. When a person uses the defense mechanism of repression, he or she _____.
    a. fails to perceive that a source of anxiety currently exists; banishes the past from present awareness
    b. banishes the past from present awareness; fails to perceive that a source of anxiety currently exists
    c. experiences the opposite of the anxiety-arousing thought or feeling; attributes the anxiety-arousing thought or feeling to someone else
    d. none of the above

    Answer: a   Page: 288
    Topic: The Expression of Impulse—Wit

Psychoanalysis after Freud

SUMMARY

Freud died more than half a century ago, but his theory lives on in a variety of ways. Some psychoanalysts try to preserve his theory in its pure form, while other post-Freudians continue to interpret, update, revise, and argue about Freud's basic theory. Others have attempted to develop their own, distinct kinds of psychoanalytic theory. Still others content themselves with debunking Freud without offering a real alternative. Neo-Freudians who have offered theories of their own include such famous individuals as Alfred Adler, Carl Jung, Karen Horney, and Erik Erikson. The kind of theoretical development these individuals worked on seems to have been relegated to the past, however. Modern psychologists interested in psychoanalysis are trying to bring rigorous research methodology to bear on some of the hundreds of hypotheses that could be derived from psychoanalytic theory. Some of these hypotheses seem to have been confirmed, such as the existence of unconscious mental processes and phenomena such as repression and transference. A particularly fruitful area of research has studied the connection between childhood patterns of attachment and adult patterns of romantic love. In the end, psychoanalysis might be best evaluated not so much in terms of the answers it has offered but of the questions it continues to raise.

ABOUT THE CHAPTER

This chapter covers a lot of ground. It summarizes the fate of psychoanalytic theory since Freud's death in 1939. It briefly describes modern, orthodox psychoanalysis and the never-ending efforts to debunk Freud. Brief summaries are included of the major neo-Freudians: Adler, Jung, Horney, and Erikson. Modern empirical research relevant to psychoanalysis is described—more here than in the First Edition. Many different examples could have been chosen for more extended treatment; I chose modern research on adult attachment theory as most likely to be of interest to a student audience.

The chapter concludes with a basically sympathetic evaluation of Freud and the contributions of psychoanalysis.

TEACHING NOTES

This chapter leaves open more possibilities than any other so far for the development of supplementary lectures. Many instructors spend major parts of the course on one or more of the neo-Freudians, particularly Jung and Erikson. Horney is not always included among this company but I recommend her highly. Her books are well written and accessible and address issues that remain relevant today. There is also something to be said for having coverage of psychoanalysis include at least one major female theorist.

My relatively extended treatment of adult attachment theory could be expanded further—the literature is huge—or supplemented by lectures on other relevant, modern research topics. These could include the cognitive unconscious, perceptual defense, the effects of psychoanalytic psychotherapy, and psychoanalytically derived personality types (such as the Jungian types measured by the Myers-Briggs Inventory). There is a renewed literature that is attempting to empirically evaluate psychoanalytic ideas, particularly the defense mechanisms (*Journal of Personality* published a special issue on this topic in 1998). Such research could be the basis of several interesting lectures. Most instructors will also want to indicate whether they think my treatment of Freud was too harsh (few will think that), too lenient, or about right.

PIECES OF THE PERSONALITY PUZZLE

Part IV of the reader includes selections by the neo-Freudian theorists Jung, Horney, and Erikson. The Erikson selection is directly relevant to material in this chapter; the others are more peripheral. It includes an evaluation of Freudian theory written more than fifty years ago (by Sears) and a more recent summary of research on defense mechanisms (by Baumeister et al.). It also includes a critique, by Crews, that illustrates the vehemence with which opponents of Freud seem to be motivated to criticize him.

DISCUSSION QUESTIONS

1. Do you think psychoanalysis overestimates the importance of sex? How important and far-reaching are the effects of sex on human life?

2. Why has psychoanalysis spawned so many vehement critics throughout its history? Is the theory so deeply flawed, or is there something—perhaps something true—about it that people find disturbing?

3. How far can psychoanalytic theory be bent and stretched before it isn't psychoanalysis any more?

4. Do you find persuasive the account of the three styles of adult attachment? Can you recognize these styles in yourself or people you know? Do you think they stem from child-rearing patterns in the way the theory describes?

5. Where, if anywhere, do you think psychoanalysis should and will go from here? Is the theory a mere historical curiosity? Or does it have a viable future?

6. Was Freud a sexist?

7. Have you found learning about psychoanalytic theory to be valuable? Is it relevant to real life?

MULTIPLE-CHOICE QUESTIONS

1. Unlike Adler and Jung, most contemporary neo-Freudians
   a. seldom have their own original theories.
   b. hold Freud's original ideas inviolate.
   c. reject most of Freud's theoretical concepts.
   d. place more emphasis on the functioning of the id than did Freud.

   Answer: a   Page: 309
   Topic: Modern Reactions to Freud

2. Most neo-Freudians rely on information from _____ to test or verify their ideas.
   a. controlled experiments
   b. archival and field studies
   c. Freud's original case descriptions
   d. patient histories and introspection

   Answer: d   Page: 310
   Topic: Neo-Freudian Issues and Theorists

3. One difference between the neo-Freudians and Freud is that nearly all neo-Freudians
   a. place more emphasis on early childhood development.
   b. put more emphasis on interpersonal relationships.
   c. adhere to evolutionary theory and emphasize the importance of sex as a motivator.
   d. emphasize the importance of unconscious processes in the determination of behavior.

   Answer: b   Page: 311
   Topic: Neo-Freudian Issues and Theorists

4. Adler felt that _____ was the prime motivator of human thought and behavior.
   a. the collective unconscious
   b. animus
   c. social interest
   d. anxiety

   Answer: c   Page: 312
   Topic: Neo-Freudian Issues and Theorists

5. Tom was a sickly child and always felt helpless. According to Adler, as an adult Tom will probably

a. be a complete invalid.
b. lose all interest in his social environment.
c. attempt to overcompensate.
d. become obsessed with his persona.

Answer: c   Page: 312
Topic: Inferiority and Compensation: Adler

6. Jane feels inferior to the people around her, but she tries to act like she is powerful and in control. Adler would say that Jane is
a. experiencing the masculine protest.
b. expressing her animus.
c. developing a persona.
d. obsessed with penis envy.

Answer: a   Page: 312
Topic: Inferiority and Compensation: Adler

7. In order for a person to develop an inferiority complex, he or she must
a. actually have some disability that makes him or her inferior to others.
b. perceive that he or she is inferior to others.
c. have parents who pushed him or her to be perfect.
d. all of the above.

Answer: b   Page: 312
Topic: Inferiority and Compensation: Adler

8. Jung believed that as the result of history, we all share inborn species-specific ideas and memories. This is Jung's idea of
a. social interests.
b. collective unconscious.
c. anima.
d. generativity.

Answer: b   Page: 313
Topic: The Collective Unconscious, Persona, and Personality: Jung

9. In Jungian terms, the recurring images that are repeated in dreams, myths, and literature throughout the world are called
a. id prototypes.
b. animus and anima.
c. personas.
d. archetypes.

Answer: d   Page: 313
Topic: The Collective Unconscious, Persona, and Personality: Jung

10. Paul is always concerned about how he appears to others so he keeps most aspects of himself hidden and puts on a carefully chosen public face in every situation. According to Jung, Paul has
    a. effectively mediated between his animus and anima.
    b. become obsessed with his persona.
    c. created a false archetype.
    d. overcompensated for his sense of inferiority.

    Answer: b   Page: 313
    Topic: The Collective Unconscious, Persona, and Personality: Jung

11. Mike's prototypical woman is sensitive and intelligent. Mike's idealized image of a woman is his
    a. unconscious compensation.
    b. animus.
    c. anima.
    d. feminine persona.

    Answer: c   Pages: 313
    Topic: The Collective Unconscious, Persona, and Personality: Jung

12. The idea that men and women each have a masculine and a feminine side is linked to Jung's ideas about
    a. intimacy and isolation.
    b. inferiority and compensation.
    c. the collective unconscious.
    d. animus and anima.

    Answer: d   Page: 313
    Topic: The Collective Unconscious, Persona, and Personality: Jung

13. Jung's distinction between people who are outwardly oriented toward the world and those who are turned in on themselves corresponds to
    a. Erikson's stage of intimacy versus isolation.
    b. Freud's ideas of the oral and anal character types.
    c. his concepts of animus and anima.
    d. the extraversion-introversion dimension of the Big Five.

    Answer: d   Page: 313
    Topic: The Collective Unconscious, Persona, and Personality: Jung

14. The Myers-Briggs Type Indicator measures
    a. the Jungian classification of the four basic ways of thinking.
    b. your prototypical images of women and men.

   c. the functioning of archetypes.

   d. aspects of Erikson's psychosocial stages of development.

Answer: a   Page: 314

Topic: The Collective Unconscious, Persona, and Personality: Jung

15. Horney's major deviation from traditional Freudian ideas was her
   a. emphasis on anxiety.
   b. view of penis envy.
   c. ideas about the development of neurotic needs.
   d. link between adult functioning and childhood struggles.

Answer: b   Page: 269

Topic: Feminine Psychology and Basic Anxiety: Horney

16. Adult behavior, according to Horney, is based on efforts to
   a. overcome the fear of being alone in a hostile world.
   b. deal with recurring Oedipal crises.
   c. resolve interpersonal conflicts with significant others.
   d. repress the collective unconscious.

Answer: a   Page: 315

Topic: Feminine Psychology and Basic Anxiety: Horney

17. Horney felt that if women experienced penis envy, it symbolized their
   a. desire to actually possess a penis.
   b. lack power and control in society.
   c. rejection of motherhood.
   d. dissatisfaction with their own bodies.

Answer: b   Pages: 314–315

Topic: Feminine Psychology and Basic Anxiety: Horney

18. Erikson's major deviation from Freud included his ideas about
   a. the functioning of the id and the physical location of libido.
   b. development as occurring in a series of stages.
   c. the function of the ego and the role of conscious conflict.
   d. the importance of parents to a child's development.

Answer: c   Page: 315

Topic: Psychosocial Development: Erikson

19. Freud's anal stage corresponds to Erikson's stage of
   a. generativity versus stagnation.
   b. basic trust versus mistrust.

    c. initiative versus guilt.

    d. autonomy versus shame and doubt.

Answer: d   Page: 316

Topic: Psychosocial Development: Erikson

20. In Erikson's view, important aspects of psychological development

    a. occur primarily in early childhood.

    b. continue to change throughout the life span.

    c. are dependent on the resolution of the Oedipal complex.

    d. involve the investment of the libido at each stage.

Answer: b   Page: 317

Topic: Psychosocial Development: Erikson

21. In middle age, we experience the psychosocial crisis of

    a. generativity versus stagnation.

    b. intimacy versus isolation.

    c. integrity versus despair.

    d. industry versus inferiority.

Answer: a   Page: 316

Topic: Psychosocial Development: Erikson

22. Ellen is a fifty-year-old woman who is raising her two grandchildren, is active in her community, and is learning how to paint. According to Erikson's theory, Ellen has chosen

    a. industry.

    b. initiative.

    c. integrity.

    d. generativity.

Answer: d   Pages: 316–317

Topic: Psychosocial Development: Erikson

23. According to Erikson, in adolescence all normal teenagers experience

    a. an inferiority complex.

    b. a struggle for intimacy.

    c. an identity crisis.

    d. a sense of shame and doubt.

Answer: c   Page: 316

Topic: Psychosocial Development: Erikson

24. In Erikson's scheme, we progress from one crisis to another according to

    a. processes of physical maturation.

b. developmental tasks at different times of life.

c. the successful repression of inappropriate id impulses.

d. the physical location of libido at each stage.

Answer: b   Page: 317
Topic: Psychosocial Development: Erikson

25. Modern developmental psychology has been most influenced by Erikson's idea that development

a. occurs in stages.

b. is influenced by parents.

c. happens across the life span.

d. is dependent on physical maturation.

Answer: c   Page: 317
Topic: Psychosocial Development: Erikson

26. Which of the following might be described as psychoanalytic research?

a. A study of the cognitive origins of aggressive behavior

b. A study to determine the impact of early child-rearing practices on adult personality characteristics

c. A study of the role of defensive optimism in maintaining health

d. All of the above

Answer: d   Page: 319
Topic: Modern Psychoanalytic Research

27. Which of the following Freudian ideas is not supported by modern research?

a. Repression works as a defense mechanism.

b. The Oedipal crisis occurs in the phallic stage.

c. Most of what the mind does is unconscious.

d. All of the above.

Answer: b   Page: 321
Topic: Modern Psychoanalytic Research

28. The psychological goal of attachment is to

a. feel secure.

b. sexually possess the parent.

c. avoid conflict with authority figures.

d. manipulate others.

Answer: a   Pages: 321–322
Topic: Attachment and Romantic Love

29. Research suggests that anxious-ambivalent children will grow up to be adults who tend to
    a. be obsessed with their romantic partners.
    b. be relatively uninterested in romantic relationships.
    c. have high self-esteem and confidence.
    d. enjoy long, stable romantic relationships.

    Answer: a   Page: 324
    Topic: Attachment and Romantic Love

30. The Freudian element that has been maintained in modern attachment theory and research is that
    a. attachments can only form between mothers and infants.
    b. the attachment bond is formed by the caregiver meeting the child's oral needs.
    c. early relationships with parents form models for later romantic attachments.
    d. attachment styles are determined by the successful resolution of the Oedipal crisis.

    Answer: c   Page: 325
    Topic: Attachment and Romantic Love

31. One criticism of psychoanalytic theory offered in the text is that it
    a. tries to explain too many things.
    b. relies too heavily on case study evidence.
    c. is so scientific that it can't be applied to daily life.
    d. bases its theorizing primarily on the experiences of women.

    Answer: b   Pages: 326–327
    Topic: Psychoanalytic Theory: An Evaluation

32. Psychoanalytic theory frequently leads to a set of hypotheses that cannot be confirmed by observations. In that respect, psychoanalytic theory
    a. is nonparsimonious.
    b. lacks generalizability.
    c. is untestable.
    d. does not use operational definitions.

    Answer: c   Pages: 327–328
    Topic: Psychoanalytic Theory: An Evaluation

33. One criticism of psychoanalytic theory is that Freud considered the development of women to be
    a. the basis of male development.
    b. a deviation from the male model.

  c. an example of normal development.
  d. a and c.

Answer: b   Page: 328
Topic: Psychoanalytic Theory: An Evaluation

34. One conclusion that can be made about psychoanalytic theory is that it is
  a. a template for what a complete theory of personality should look like.
  b. an example of the problems associated with basing a theory on experimental evidence.
  c. valuable for the insights it has provided about women's development.
  d. scientifically based and therefore valid and generalizable to most people.

Answer: a   Page: 328
Topic: Psychoanalytic Theory: An Evaluation

SUMMARY

The phenomenological approach to personality concentrates on the experience, or phenomenology, of being alive and aware from moment to moment. This emphasis makes the approach humanistic, because it concentrates on that which makes the study of humans different from the study of objects or animals. Wilhelm Wundt founded the first psychological laboratory in history in an attempt to formulate a phenomenological chemistry, a science that would describe all the elements of experience. Phenomenology is closely related to the philosophical school called existentialism, which breaks experience into three parts (of the world, of others, and of one's own experience), claims that a close analysis of existence implies that it has no meaning beyond what we give it, and concludes that a failure to face this fact constitutes living in bad faith. It also asserts that each moment of experience is all that matters; this implies that individuals have free will and that the only way to understand another person is to understand his or her experience of the world. The approach of Zen Buddhism is very different and teaches that the existence and isolation of the single human soul is merely an illusion. All persons are part of a larger, interconnected universe. True enlightenment entails awareness that the present moment is no more real or important than any other and that other people are just as important as oneself. To achieve such enlightenment is to experience nirvana.

Humanist psychologists such as Rogers, Maslow, and Kelly seem to mix some of this Eastern optimism into their brand of existentialism. Rogers and Maslow asserted that a person who faces his or her experience directly can become a fully functioning person; Rogers believed this outcome could only occur for individuals who had received unconditional positive regard from the important people in their lives. Kelly's theory says that each person's experience of the world is organized by a unique set of personal constructs, or general themes. Scientific paradigms have much in common with these personal constructs. Csikszentmihalyi's recent theory says that the best state of existence is to be in a state of flow, in which challenges and capabilities are well balanced. Although modern humanistic psychology continues to maintain that the rest of psychology makes a fundamental mistake by ignoring that which makes humans unique among objects of study, the field has so far largely offered only nonrigorous, introspective accounts, which psychologists with a scientific approach find unconvincing. Humanistic psychologists must be given credit for providing the only approach that still even attempts to address the mystery of human experience and awareness. The phenomenological approach continues to have an important impact on the practice of psychotherapy, on modern cognitive views of personality, and on the study of psychology across cultures.

ABOUT THE CHAPTER

The term *humanistic psychology* is often used but it is not always clear what it means. The interpretation offered in this chapter is that humanistic psychology is an approach rooted in existential philosophy, especially existentialism's emphasis on phenomenology. This trio of multisyllabic terms—*existentialism, phenomenology,* and *humanism*—may seem forbidding at first, but the chapter tries to present the essence of each concept and its interrelations as clearly as possible.

New in the Second Edition is that the phenomenological approach is framed from the outset in terms of Wilhelm Wundt's phenomenology. Wundt isn't usually considered a humanist, but he did focus on the nature of experience, something that only the humanists still see as the central concern of psychology. Also new is the discussion of the eastern philosophy Zen Buddhism. Among other purposes, it serves to illustrate an important point: While the arguments of European existentialists can appear completely compelling, they are cogently opposed on nearly every point by an ancient perspective originating on the other side of the world. This point can provide a nice bridge to the next chapter (on cross-cultural studies).

TEACHING NOTES

One challenge in teaching this material is to find a way for students not to be immediately turned off by the philosophic terminology. It helps, I think, to emphasize that existentialism is a concern with the meaning of life, that phenomenology concerns how it feels to be alive, and that humanism emphasizes whatever is seen as distinctive about humanity.

This chapter probably contains enough existential philosophy for any personality course. An interested instructor with relevant expertise might wish to expand on the treatment of Rogers, Maslow, or Kelly. In particular, Rogers continues to influence the practice of psychotherapy. Maslow's theory is widely applied to industrial settings (e.g., in models of worker motivation). Kelly's phenomenological approach is an important underpinning of the modern cognitive approaches to be considered in later chapters (Walter Mischel was a student of Kelly!). An instructor familiar with eastern philosophy might wish to illustrate how it contrasts with European existentialism, while also apparently being present in the background of American humanism. All of these points would be worth emphasizing and expanding in lecture.

PIECES OF THE PERSONALITY PUZZLE

Part V of the reader begins with a surprisingly readable primer on existential philosopher by Jean-Paul Sartre. The presentation of Sartre in this chapter is largely based on this reading. The reader also includes selections by the U.S. humanists Maslow and Rogers, both of whom are discussed in this chapter. The chapter considers Csikszentmihalyi's theory of flow; an excerpt from one of his articles on the subject is included in the reader. Perhaps the most unusual selection in the reader is the piece by Gordon Allport, whose role as an important humanistic theorist seems almost forgotten by modern psychologists.

DISCUSSION QUESTIONS

1. What would Wilhelm Wundt think about the direction of modern psychology? Would he think it ignores key issues?

2. Do people have free will? Or are they driven by their reinforcement history, unconscious motivations, and trait structures? If free will exists, what exactly does this mean and how is it possible?

3. What does it feel like to be alive and aware? Can it be described in words? Can psychology address this experience? How?

4. How can a person decide between right and wrong? Is there some authority we can turn to? If someone mentions God, how do you decide what God wants you to do? How do you decide whether or not to obey God? (Needless to say, be careful with this line of discussion, it can be emotionally loaded for many students.)

5. Sartre believed God does not exist but said that even if God did exist, it wouldn't matter. What did Sartre mean by this?

6. Are people really forever alone and closed off from each other, as the European existentialists said? Or is this separateness an illusion, as Zen Buddhism would claim?

7. How do you think Rogers and Maslow were able to start with existentialist ideas and develop such optimistic-sounding psychologies?

8. If a psychotherapist is treating a murderer or child molester, do you think the therapist should give the client unconditional positive regard? Why or why not?

9. Would you spend your whole life in "flow" if you could?

MULTIPLE-CHOICE QUESTIONS

1. Your unique, individual experience of the world is called your
   a. humanism.
   b. phenomenology.
   c. Umwelt.
   d. existentialism.

   Answer: b   Page: 331
   Topic: Experience and Awareness

2. Adherents to the phenomenological approach believe that
   a. behavior is primarily determined by early events.
   b. to understand the individual, you must understand his or her unconscious and hidden motives.
   c. the methods that are used to study other scientific phenomena can be applied to the study of the mind.
   d. the study of the human mind is affected by human awareness.

   Answer: d   Pages: 335–336
   Topic: A Humanistic Psychology

3. Phenomenological, existential, and humanistic psychologists all agree
   a. that psychology should focus on conscious experience.
   b. that the study of human beings is fundamentally different from the study of anything else.
   c. that human beings possess free will.
   d. all of the above.

   Answer: d   Page: 339
   Topic: A Diverse Approach

4. The phenomenological approach claims that your behavior is the result of your
   a. history of reinforcement.
   b. future aspirations and goals.
   c. immediate conscious experience.
   d. cultural traditions.

   Answer: c   Page: 339
   Topic: Awareness is Everything

5. Trait, psychoanalytic, and behavioral psychologists agree that behavior is _____ while phenomenologists claim it is _____.
   a. determined; freely chosen
   b. motivated by unconscious desires; driven by conscious motives

c. inconsistent; consistent
d. caused by external factors; caused by internal states

Answer: a   Page: 340
Topic: Free Will

6. Your particular freely chosen interpretations of reality are called your
   a. Mitwelt.
   b. construals.
   c. needs.
   d. experiential definitions.

Answer: b   Page: 341
Topic: Free Will

7. According to the phenomenological perspective, to understand another person, you must understand his or her
   a. unconscious desires.
   b. goals and aspirations.
   c. construals.
   d. Mitwelt.

Answer: c   Page: 341
Topic: Understanding Others

8. One possible interpretation of the basic phenomenological philosophy is that
   a. objective reality exists for diverse groups of people and different cultures.
   b. all interpretations of reality are equally valid.
   c. if you look at the world through another's eyes you will realize your own world view is invalid.
   d. our behavior, thoughts, and feelings are determined by past experience.

Answer: b   Page: 341
Topic: Understanding Others

9. The key existential question is:
   a. What is the meaning of existence?
   b. What is the nature of existence?
   c. How does existence feel?
   d. All of the above are key questions.

Answer: d   Page 342
Topic: Existentialism

10. _____ consists of your biological experiences and _____ consists of your psychological experiences.

a. Umwelt; Eigenwelt
b. Mitwelt; Umwelt
c. Eigenwelt; Mitwelt
d. Umwelt; Mitwelt

Answer: a   Pages: 342–343
Topic: Three Parts of Experience

11. Carolyn is fondly thinking about her mother. Carolyn is experiencing
    a. self-actualization.
    b. Mitwelt.
    c. Eigenwelt.
    d. angst.

    Answer: b   Page: 342
    Topic: Three Parts of Experience

12. The time, place, and circumstances into which you were born is called your
    a. existential location.
    b. Eigenwelt.
    c. thrown-ness.
    d. angst.

    Answer: c   Page: 343
    Topic: "Thrown-ness" and Angst

13. Jerry has been wondering what life means and whether he is living his life
    purposefully. If he cannot answer these questions, he will probably experience
    a. Eigenwelt.
    b. thrown-ness.
    c. angst.
    d. self-actualization.

    Answer: c   Page: 343
    Topic: "Thrown-ness" and Angst

14. _____ is the anxiety that results from contemplation of existential
    concerns.
    a. Thrown-ness
    b. Umwelt
    c. Construal
    d. Angst

    Answer: d   Page: 343
    Topic: "Thrown-ness" and Angst

15. Mike thinks that sitting around contemplating the meaning of existence is a waste of time. He spends his life concentrating on developing his career, building a bigger house for his family, and enjoying himself. Sartre and other existentialists would say Mike is
    a. living in bad faith.
    b. a fully functioning person.
    c. striving to meet his social needs.
    d. unlikely to experience flow.

    Answer: a   Page: 344
    Topic: Bad Faith

16. Existentialists would say that if Donna doesn't worry about existential concerns but instead focuses on getting a job, establishing relationships with others, and raising her family she will
    a. become a fully functioning person.
    b. experience authentic existence.
    c. still not be happy.
    d. feel angst.

    Answer: c   Pages: 344–345
    Topic: Bad Faith

17. Steven has come to terms with his mortality, accepted responsibility for his existence, and knows that he determines what happens in his life. Existentialists would say that Steven is
    a. living in bad faith.
    b. experiencing thrown-ness.
    c. attaining authentic existence.
    d. achieving Mitwelt.

    Answer: c   Pages: 345–346
    Topic: Authentic Existence

18. According to Sartre, the existential challenge is to
    a. avoid thinking about the meaning of existence.
    b. face the basic uncertainty and anguish of life and find meaning.
    c. maintain generativity and avoid stagnation.
    d. become a fully functioning, self-actualizing person.

    Answer: b   Page: 346
    Topic: Authentic Existence

19. Carl Rogers maintained that the one basic tendency for humans was to
    a. maintain and enhance life.
    b. struggle against despair and anguish.

c. identify personal constructs.

d. develop conditions of worth.

Answer: a   Page: 349
Topic: Existential Optimism: Rogers and Maslow

20. Rogers's idea of actualization is similar to Freud's concept of
    a. Thanatos.
    b. ego.
    c. libido.
    d. intellectualization.

Answer: c   Page: 349
Topic: Existential Optimism: Rogers and Maslow

21. Linda thinks that her friends will only like her if she is thin, attractive, and cheerful. Rogers would say that it is unlikely that Linda will
    a. develop conditions of worth.
    b. become a fully functioning person.
    c. build personal constructs.
    d. experience angst.

Answer: b   Page: 349
Topic: Existential Optimism: Rogers and Maslow

22. To avoid developing conditions of worth, a person should experience _____ from the important people in his or her life.
    a. unconditional positive regard
    b. Mitwelt
    c. conditions of worth
    d. existential optimism

Answer: a   Pages: 349–350
Topic: Existential Optimism: Rogers and Maslow

23. The fundamental belief of humanism is that
    a. unconscious experience determines behavior.
    b. people are basically good.
    c. human beings are superior to other organisms.
    d. accurate perceptions of the world cause neurotic distortions.

Answer: b   Page: 350
Topic: Existential Optimism: Rogers and Maslow

24. The theories of Rogers and Maslow imply that if you leave human beings alone, they will
    a. develop into healthy and happy people.
    b. suffer anguish and despair.

c. develop conditions of worth.

d. experience neurotic distortions of the world.

Answer: a   Page: 350

Topic: Existential Optimism: Rogers and Maslow

25. Research findings indicate that one result of Rogerian psychotherapy may be that

a. people become more like their ideal self.

b. people establish their own conditions of worth.

c. clients report feeling more despair and anguish.

d. most clients achieve self-actualization through therapy.

Answer: a   Page: 351

Topic: Existential Optimism: Rogers and Maslow

26. A difficulty in determining the effect of Rogerian psychotherapy is

a. that it is not clear that the match between perceived self and ideal self is an adequate criteria for psychological adjustment.

b. that the criterion used for determining adjustment could lead us to perceive people with obvious disorders as being well adjusted.

c. that the results may be due to clients' changing their ideal views.

d. All of the above are difficulties.

Answer: d   Page: 351

Topic: Existential Optimism: Rogers and Maslow

27. Kelly's personal construct theory emphasizes that individuals

a. construct reality through neurotic distortions.

b. build our experience of reality through unique sets of ideas about the world.

c. construct a hierarchy of needs that motivate behavior.

d. build an authentic existence through the acceptance of personal responsibility.

Answer: b   Pages: 351–352

Topic: Personal Constructs: Kelly

28. A personality test that asks you to identify sets of three people, ideas, or objects and then has you describe how any two of them are similar to each other and different from the third is attempting to assess your

a. hierarchy of needs.

b. conditions of worth.

c. cognitive scripts.

d. personal constructs.

Answer: d   Page: 352

Topic: Personal Constructs: Kelly

144 | *Chapter 13*

29. Csikszentimihalyi's concept of flow is analogous to
    a. self-actualization.
    b. an authentic existence.
    c. an optimal experience.
    d. existential optimism.

    Answer: c   Page: 355
    Topic: Flow: Csikszentimihalyi

30. You are most likely to experience flow if the activity you are doing is
    a. easy.
    b. confusing.
    c. challenging.
    d. boring.

    Answer: c   Page: 356
    Topic: Flow: Csikszentimihalyi

31. Research indicates that experiencing flow tends to
    a. elevate mood.
    b. create anxiety.
    c. slow metabolism.
    d. decrease activity levels.

    Answer: a   Page: 356
    Topic: Flow: Csikszentimihalyi

32. Currently, humanistic research most frequently consists of
    a. experimental examinations of construals.
    b. subjective analyses of experience.
    c. correlational field studies.
    d. systematic behavior analysis.

    Answer: b   Page: 357
    Topic: Humanistic Psychology Today

33. Phenomenologists tend to disagree among themselves about
    a. the existence of free will.
    b. the importance of immediate experience.
    c. whether awareness makes the human mind unique.
    d. whether the human condition is basically positive or negative.

    Answer: d   Page: 360
    Topic: On Happiness

34. Imagine that you are participating in a psychology experiment. The experimenter asks you to take a bite of chocolate and describe your experience of the chocolate—its tastes, its texture, its feel on your tongue, and so on. You would be involved in which method of psychological research?
    a. Experimental
    b. Correlational
    c. Introspection
    d. L data

    Answer: c   Page: 336
    Topic: Wilhlem Wundt's Phenomenology

35. In his pioneering studies of phenomenology, Wilhlem Wundt attempted
    a. to describe what went on in a person's mind when he or she felt various sensations and came to simple decisions.
    b. to identify the basic elements of perception and thought.
    c. to analyze an experience, thought, or feeling into its most basic, irreducible parts.
    d. all of the above.

    Answer: d   Page: 337
    Topic: Wilhlem Wundt's Phenomenology

36. Wilhelm Wundt's research on phenomenology encountered what difficulty?
    a. Its practical and theoretical implications were unclear.
    b. The method of introspection was deemed unsatisfactory
    c. Wundt neglected people's internal experiences in favor of observable behaviors.
    d. a and b.

    Answer: d   Pages: 357–358
    Topic: Wilhlem Wundt's Phenomenology

37. In characterizing the human experience, the traditional Western philosophical perspective emphasizes the _____, while the Zen Buddhist perspective emphasizes the _____.
    a. interconnectedness of everyone and everything across time; experience of a single individual at a single moment in time
    b. experience of a single individual at a single moment in time; interconnectedness of everyone and everything across time
    c. phenomenological method of experience; empirical method of experience
    d. a and c

    Answer: b   Pages: 346–347
    Topic: The Eastern Alternative: Zen Buddhism

<table>
<tr><td>**CHAPTER 14**</td><td>Cultural Variation in Experience, Behavior, and Personality</td></tr>
</table>

OUTLINE

SUMMARY

If, as the phenomenologists claim, a person's construal of the world is all-important, a logical next question concerns the ways in which such construals of reality vary across different cultures. This topic is addressed by cross-cultural psychology. It is important to know whether psychological research and theorizing that originates in one culture can be applied to another, because misunderstandings across cultures can lead to conflict and even war and because to understand how other peoples view reality can expand our own understanding of the world. Hazards of cross-cultural research include ethnocentrism, outgroup bias, and the unfortunate fact that ultimately one person can never fully comprehend the experience of another.

Some psychologists ignore cross-cultural issues. A second group, the deconstructionists, argues that comparing cultures is impossible; we must seek to understand each culture in its own terms. Some deconstructionists have even claimed that the Western sense of self is a cultural artifact. A third group of psychologists follows a comparative approach, contrasting etics, or elements that all cultures have in common, with emics, or elements that make them different. Cultures have been compared on emic dimensions including complexity, tightness, and collectivism. Deconstructionists avoid the question of where these differences originate, but one comparative approach sees the ultimate origin of cultural differences in the differing ecologies to which groups around the world must adapt. Despite the importance of cross-cultural psychology, it is important to bear in mind that individuals vary within as well as across cultures, that cultural relativism can be taken too far, and that beneath all cultural differences there may be a universal human condition in an existential sense: the need to exist, to work, to relate to other people, and ultimately to die.

ABOUT THE CHAPTER

The location of this chapter, in the same section as humanistic psychology, is somewhat unusual. But I believe that the essential aspect of humanism is its phenomenological orientation and that the basic question of cross-cultural psychology is also phenomenological: Do members of different cultures see the world in a fundamentally different way? The continuation of the phenomenological theme across Chapters 13 and 14 is what ties them together. And to bring the presentation full circle, Chapter 14 ends with a quote from Jean-Paul Sartre, considered near the beginning of Chapter 13.

TEACHING NOTES

This is material that students usually find interesting. A point I have learned to keep in mind when teaching this material is that it is too easy to spend one's lecture time talking about abstractions. The comparability of cultures, phenomenology, and deconstructionism versus realism are all interesting ideas that can be developed at length. But if these issues are overemphasized, one can finish the cross-cultural part of the course without having mentioned an actual difference between cultures! For this reason, in every revision of this chapter I found myself putting in more specific examples of cross-cultural variation, and I try to remember to do the same in lecture.

I am no world traveler but have lived in northern and southern California, in New England, in the Midwest, and for a short time in New Zealand. I draw on this experience for examples in this chapter. An instructor who has lived in other parts of the world could probably provide even better examples. Students—especially those who might be from other cultures—can also be a source of good examples from their experience and often enjoy providing them. Students who belong to ethnic minorities should also be encouraged to describe the ways in which mainstream psychology does or does not apply to themselves and the people they know.

A fair portion of this chapter ventures into the debate between deconstructionism and realism. Deconstructionism is of course a widespread viewpoint in other parts of academia, especially literature departments, but has barely affected psychology. To the extent the instructor or students have expertise in these other areas, an interesting and more general discussion of the construction of reality—inside and outside of psychology—might be possible.

Obviously my own position on this issue is that of a realist. An instructor who disagrees on this point could construct an interesting and useful lecture about how and why.

The chapter discusses the debate over abortion rights in the context of contrasting the individualist and collectivist viewpoints. This is hazardous material, of course; some students will find it emotionally involving. A class debate on this subject might easily generate more heat than light; I am not sure I would recommend it. The comments in the text are meant to be neutral and designed to point out only why reasonable compromise is so difficult.

Finally, I would urge instructors of this material to underline for their students the phenomenological theme that ties together Chapters 13 and 14: It is one's experience of the world that is all-important, and to understand other people, we must understand their points of view even if—especially if—they are very different from our own.

PIECES OF THE PERSONALITY PUZZLE

All the selections in Part VI of the reader are directly relevant to this chapter. The reader includes two cross-cultural investigations of personality, one (tongue in cheek) by the anthropologist Miner and the other by the psychologists Yang and

Bond. It also includes an argument for the important of cultural differences within national boundaries, by Cohen et al. and by Murray et al. The reader includes an excerpt from the article by Markus and Kitayama discussed here and Triandis's major theoretical paper, which presents the three dimensions of cultural variation summarized in this chapter.

DISCUSSION QUESTIONS

1. Have you ever lived in a different culture or known well someone from a different culture? Do people in that other culture view things differently? How fundamental are these differences?

2. If you wanted to really understand another culture, such as on an island in the South Pacific, what would you have to do? How could you be sure your interpretation of that culture was correct?

3. Have you encountered the concept of deconstructionism in courses or in your reading? How was it presented in that other context? What do you think about it?

4. What are the pros and cons of living in an individualist versus a collectivist culture? Which do you think you would prefer? Is your preference a result of your own cultural conditioning?

5. What do you think is more important: The differences between cultures or the differences among individuals within cultures?

6. Consider the example, presented in the text, of the practice of female genital mutilation. Can we judge this practice as wrong? On what grounds—if any—can we judge the practices of another culture as moral or immoral?

MULTIPLE-CHOICE QUESTIONS

1. Your text suggests that cross-cultural differences in experience, personality, and behavior essentially reflect
   a. different cultural construals of reality.
   b. varying degrees of psychological adjustment across cultures.
   c. maladaptive parenting styles in non-Western cultures.
   d. deconstructionist tendencies in collectivist cultures.

   Answer: a   Page: 363
   Topic: Cultural Variations in Experience, Personality, and Behavior

2. Psychologists who are concerned that the results of contemporary empirical research may not apply to all of humanity are questioning the _____ of those results.

a. reliability
b. generalizability
c. cross-cultural flexibility
d. construct validity

Answer: b   Page: 364
Topic: The Importance of Cross-cultural Differences

3. It has been suggested that the only real way that psychologists can address the generalizability issue is to
a. conduct research using subjects from around the world.
b. limit their focus to one homogeneous sample at a time.
c. subtract the effects of culture from their research findings.
d. repeat their studies in carefully controlled laboratory settings.

Answer: a   Page: 364
Topic: The Importance of Cross-cultural Differences

4. It is important to identify cross-cultural differences in experience, personality, and behavior because
a. the differences, if not understood, may cause misunderstandings.
b. such differences tell us about the variability in human experience.
c. cross-cultural research informs us about the generalizability of research findings.
d. all of the above.

Answer: d   Pages: 364–367
Topic: The Importance of Cross-cultural Differences

5. If two cultures experience the same emotions, seek the same goals, and organize their thoughts in comparable ways, then the two cultures
a. are individualistic cultures.
b. have collectivist construals.
c. have "experience near" constructs.
d. view the world through culture-free lenses.

Answer: c   Page: 367
Topic: The Importance of Cross-cultural Differences

6. Ethnocentrism is the tendency to
a. see members of groups we don't belong to as all being alike.
b. judge another culture from the point of view of our own.
c. see members of our own ethnic group as all being very different from one another.
d. limit the focus of cross-cultural research by studying one group at a time.

Answer: b   Page: 367
Topic: Ethnocentrism

7. We are most likely to commit ethnocentrism when the "real" nature of the situation
   a. is difficult to understand.
   b. directly affects us.
   c. seems very obvious.
   d. does not involve us.

   Answer: c   Page: 368
   Topic: Ethnocentrism

8. A U.S. psychologist is using an assessment device called the Strange Situation to measure the quality of an infant's attachment to its mother. Experience tells him that U.S. babies who have developed secure attachments usually cry when they are left alone and immediately run to their mother when she returns. However, he has recently found that German babies do not appear upset by their mother's departure and frequently ignore her when she returns. His conclusion that these German babies have not formed secure attachments to their mothers may be colored by
   a. ethnocentrism.
   b. racism.
   c. the outgroup homogeneity bias.
   d. deconstructionism.

   Answer: a   Pages: 367–369
   Topic: Ethnocentrism

9. The tendency to see members of your own group as being very different from one another but the members of groups you don't belong to as being very similar to each other is called the
   a. ethnocentric error.
   b. in-group favoritism bias.
   c. outgroup homogeneity bias.
   d. cultural diversity error.

   Answer: c   Page: 369
   Topic: Outgroup Bias

10. John thinks that women are pretty much all alike whereas men are quite different from one another. John's beliefs about men and women reflect
    a. the outgroup homogeneity bias.
    b. an incomplete gender categorization.
    c. ethnocentrism.
    d. the etics of gender.

    Answer: a   Page: 369
    Topic: Outgroup Bias

11. "The individualistic society of the Xanus appreciates the fundamental tendency for human beings to develop a unique sense of self and thus allows them to develop an advanced type of self esteem that is not possible in the less-advanced collectivist cultures." This statement would most likely be made by a researcher who
    a. adopted a deconstructivist point of view.
    b. had gone native and romanticized the culture being studied.
    c. conducted research by 747.
    d. had conducted an idiographic assessment.

    Answer: b   Pages: 369–370
    Topic: Going Native

12. Among psychologists, the most common approach to cross-cultural issues is to
    a. adopt idiographic assessment strategies.
    b. claim that comparisons are impossible because no common frame of reference exists.
    c. compare different cultures along common dimensions.
    d. ignore them.

    Answer: d   Page: 371
    Topic: Ignoring Cross-cultural Issues

13. The intellectual approach of _____ is the basis of cultural psychology's claim that there is no culture-free way to look at any culture and that all cultural views of reality are equally valid.
    a. ethnocentrism
    b. deconstructionism
    c. ecological realism
    d. collectivism

    Answer: b   Page: 371
    Topic: Deconstructionism

14. The _____ capacity is the human capacity to invent and use symbol systems.
    a. emic
    b. etic
    c. semiotic
    d. artifactual

    Answer: c   Page: 372
    Topic: Deconstructionism—The Semiotic Subject

15. Some cultural psychologists may see people as being _____ who do not have traits, mental states, or psychological processes that are independent of culture.
    a. semiotic subjects
    b. emic individuals
    c. culture-free collectivists
    d. individualistic systems

    Answer: a   Page: 372
    Topic: Deconstructionism—The Semiotic Subject

16. The deconstructionist approach to cultural psychology claims that
    a. psychological processes are universal.
    b. cultures should be compared on common dimensions.
    c. each culture must be examined in its own terms.
    d. idiographic assessments are the only culture-free method of studying groups.

    Answer: c   Pages: 372–373
    Topic: Deconstructionism—The Semiotic Subject

17. Shweder and Bourne (1982) asked Hindu and U.S. informants to describe people they knew. The Americans tended to use trait terms like "He is kind" about 50 percent of the time, while the Hindus were more likely to use descriptive contextualized phrases like "He has trouble giving things to his family." How would deconstructionist cultural psychologists interpret these findings?
    a. The idea that people possess personality traits is likely an arbitrary social construction.
    b. Hindus do not have conceptions of each others' personality traits.
    c. Both Americans and Hindus understand the concept of traits but may differ in how they use trait terms.
    d. a and b.

    Answer: d   Pages: 373–375
    Topic: Deconstructionism—The Indian Sense of Self

18. The point that cultures cannot be compared or classified on common dimensions because those dimensions may not be relevant to all cultures resembles Allport's argument in favor of
    a. idiographic assessment of individuals.
    b. development of culture-free tests.
    c. nomothetic assessment of people.
    d. semiotic analysis of groups.

    Answer: a   Pages: 375–376
    Topic: Deconstructionism—On Categorization

19. According to one view, one of the most-devastating difficulties with a deconstructionist approach to studying cultural variation is that it
    a. comes very close to making cross-cultural psychology impossible.
    b. focuses too much on comparisons across different cultures.
    c. does not allow researchers to understand cultures in their own terms.
    d. all of the above.

    Answer: a   Page: 376
    Topic: Deconstructionism—On Categorization

20. The _____ approach to research on cultural variation involves classifying cultures along common dimensions and studying their similarities and differences.
    a. deconstructionist cultural
    b. comparative cultural
    c. collectivist
    d. structural

    Answer: b   Pages: 376–377
    Topic: The Comparative Cultural Approach

21. Components of ideas that are particular to a specific culture are called _____ and components that are universal across cultures are called _____.
    a. individualisms; collectivisms
    b. emics; etics
    c. cultures; values
    d. etics; emics

    Answer: b   Page: 377
    Topic: Emics and Etics

22. The finding that the Big Five personality factors can be identified cross-culturally if one allows for some variation of the specific traits that make up each of the Big Five is closely related to the idea(s) of _____ in the comparative cultural approach.
    a. deconstructionism
    b. collectivism versus individualism
    c. tightness versus looseness
    d. emics and etics

    Answer: d   Page: 377
    Topic: Emics and Etics

23. Triandis has proposed that cultures vary along which of the following dimensions?

a. Tightness versus looseness
b. Complexity
c. Individualism and collectivism
d. All of the above

Answer: d   Pages: 379–384
Topic: Differences among Cultures

24. If less than 2 percent of a country's population exhibited left-handedness, then Triandis would say that the culture was likely
a. a tight culture.
b. a simple culture.
c. a collectivist culture.
d. an easy culture.

Answer: a   Page: 380
Topic: Differences among Cultures.

25. Research indicates that people in _____ cultures tend to strictly observe social hierarchies while those in _____ cultures are less attentive to differences in status.
a. tight; loose
b. collectivist; individualistic
c. simple; complex
d. tough; easy

Answer: b   Page: 382
Topic: Differences among Cultures

26. Research comparing individualistic and collectivist cultures has found that in individualistic cultures people are more likely to
a. emphasize obligations, reciprocity, and duty to others.
b. be right handed.
c. marry for love.
d. be ethnically homogeneous.

Answer: c   Page: 382
Topic: Differences among Cultures

27. Cultural tightness is analogous to the personality traits of
a. idiocentrism and allocentrism.
b. conscientiousness and intolerance for ambiguity.
c. extraversion and introversion.
d. neuroticism and emotional stability.

Answer: b   Page: 384
Topic: Differences among Cultures

28. In Triandis's model, the distinctive tasks a culture has needed to accomplish and the physical layout and resources of its land are called the culture's
    a. ecology.
    b. complexity.
    c. socialization processes.
    d. personality.

    Answer: a   Pages: 385–386
    Topic: The Ecological Approach

29. Differences in ecology can result in differences in
    a. the personality of the area's inhabitants.
    b. the tightness versus looseness of the culture.
    c. the collectivism or individualism of the culture.
    d. all of the above.

    Answer: d   Page: 386
    Topic: The Ecological Approach

30. The view in cross-cultural psychology that variations between cultures are more important than variations between people within a culture is a _____ view.
    a. collectivist
    b. individualistic
    c. ecological
    d. relativist

    Answer: a   Page: 387
    Topic: Implications of Cultural Psychology

31. Psychologists frequently assume that while there may be considerable variation in _____ across cultures, genders, social classes, and ethnic groups, _____ can be considered universal.
    a. process; content
    b. content; process
    c. attitudes; values
    d. values; attitudes

    Answer: b   Page: 389
    Topic: Implications of Cultural Psychology

32. One existential view is that the universal human condition is the need to
    a. exist, work, relate to others, and die.
    b. develop a sense of self and conditions of worth.
    c. think, feel, and behave.
    d. pursue personal projects.

    Answer: a   Page: 389
    Topic: The Implications of Cultural Psychology

CHAPTER 15

How the World Creates Who You Are: Behaviorism and the View from Outside

OUTLINE

SUMMARY

Behaviorism's key tenet is that we can only know about what we can see, and we can see everything we need in know. This translates to a basic belief that all behavior is a function of the rewards and punishments in one's past and present

157

environment, and figuring out how behavior is a function of the environment is called a functional analysis. The philosophical roots of behaviorism include *empiricism,* a belief that all knowledge comes from experience; *associationism,* a belief that two stimuli paired together will come to be seen as one; *hedonism,* the belief that the goal of life is gentle pleasure; and *utilitarianism,* the belief that the most important test of a psychological idea is whether it works for behavioral change. In behaviorist terminology, learning is any change in behavior as a result of experience. Basic principles of learning include habituation, classical conditioning, and operant conditioning. Classical conditioning affects emotions and feelings; operant conditioning affects behavior. Key figures in the development of operant conditioning include Edward Thorndike, Clark Hull, and B. F. Skinner. Punishment is a useful technique of operant conditioning if it is applied correctly, which it almost never is. Behaviorism has contributed a useful technology of behavioral change and forced the rest of the field to clarify and defend its use of mentalistic concepts (such as thought and mind). But behaviorism neglects important topics such as motivation, emotion, and cognition. The social learning theories, considered in the next chapter, have as their goal the addition of such phenomena to behaviorism.

ABOUT THE CHAPTER

Much of this chapter is a review of basic principles of classical and operant conditioning that most students should have learned earlier—and perhaps remembered—from their introductory psychology course. The only distinctive point made here is my claim that classical conditioning better explains emotions, and operant conditioning better explains behavior. The chapter also contains a detailed presentation on how to punish correctly, included because I think it contains some useful advice for future parents and managers from a behavioral perspective.

TEACHING NOTES

Because much of this material should at least sound familiar to students, they should not find it difficult. If students *are* unfamiliar with basic behavioral principles (such as extinction, schedules of reinforcement, and so on) then their summary in this chapter is probably inadequate and will need to be augmented in lecture.

PIECES OF THE PERSONALITY PUZZLE

Part VII of the reader includes material from this and the next two chapters, and is designed to show the progression of thought from behaviorism to social learning theory to the modern cognitive approaches. For this chapter, the first two selections in Part VII (both by Skinner) are directly relevant.

DISCUSSION QUESTIONS

1. Does all knowledge come from experience? Where else could it come from?

2. Why do people do anything? What makes a reward rewarding and a punishment punishing?

3. What do you think about the behaviorist idea that it is enough for psychology to be able to predict and to control behavior and that it is unnecessary (and impossible) to know about what goes on inside the mind? Does psychology need to address the inner workings of the mind? Why?

4. Consider the text's discussion of punishment. Do you think punishment is too dangerous to use at all? Given the difficulties, when—if ever—is its use appropriate?

MULTIPLE-CHOICE QUESTIONS

1. Behaviorists believe that all of the important causes of behavior can be found in an individual's
   a. unconscious mind.
   b. conscious mind.
   c. personality traits.
   d. environment.

   Answer: d   Page: 397
   Topic: How the World Creates Who You Are

2. Behaviorists assert that personality and all of its causes can be directly observed by looking at a person's
   a. environment.
   b. conscious mind.
   c. behavior.
   d. a and c.

   Answer: d   Page: 398
   Topic: How the World Creates Who You Are

3. The behaviorists' attempt to determine how behavior is connected to the environment is called
   a. functional analysis.
   b. empiricism.
   c. associationism.
   d. behavioral linking.

   Answer: a   Page: 398
   Topic: Functional Analysis

4. According to behaviorism, what is the connector between the stimuli of the environment and the person's behavior?
   a. Cognition
   b. Learning
   c. Motivation
   d. Affect

   Answer: b   Page: 398
   Topic: Functional Analysis

5. Behaviorism has its philosophical roots in
   a. associationism.
   b. empiricism.
   c. hedonism.
   d. all of the above.

   Answer: d   Page: 399
   Topic: The Philosophical Roots of Behaviorism

6. The basic idea behind empiricism is
   a. two things become linked mentally if they are experienced close together in time.
   b. the structure of the mind determines our experience of reality.
   c. everything we know is the result of our experience with reality.
   d. every large phenomenon can be understood by breaking it down into smaller components.

   Answer: c   Page: 399
   Topic: The Philosophical Roots of Behaviorism—Empiricism

7. John Locke's conception of the newborn mind as a tabula rasa is closely associated with the idea of
   a. associationism.
   b. empiricism.
   c. rationalism.
   d. reductionism.

   Answer: b   Page: 399
   Topic: The Philosophical Roots of Behaviorism—Empiricism

8. If a particular song frequently precedes being touched by your significant other, then eventually hearing the song will make you think of being touched by him or her. This is the basic idea behind
   a. reductionism.
   b. habituation.

c. associationism.

d. hedonism.

Answer: c   Pages: 399–400
Topic: The Philosophical Roots of Behaviorism—Associationism

9. The idea that personality could be best understood if you could break it down into specific neural mechanisms and discrete biological processes is linked to

a. associationism.

b. reductionism.

c. utilitarianism.

d. functional analysis.

Answer: b   Page: 401
Topic: The Philosophical Roots of Behaviorism—Associationism

10. Hedonism provides the _____ necessary for learning and behavior to occur.

a. motivation

b. cognition

c. emotion

d. knowledge

Answer: a   Page: 401
Topic: The Philosophical Roots of Behaviorism—Hedonism

11. When the new mobile is first hung over her crib, baby Jessica looks at it frequently. After several weeks pass, she spends hardly any time looking at the mobile. Jessica has become _____ to the mobile.

a. classically conditioned

b. operantly conditioned

c. habituated

d. counterconditioned

Answer: c   Page: 403
Topic: Three Kinds of Learning—Habituation

12. In Pavlov's famous studies, when presentation of meat was frequently preceded by the sound of a bell, the dogs

a. refused to eat the meat.

b. began to salivate at the sound of the bell.

c. showed fear responses to the bell.

d. salivated only when actually given the meat.

Answer: b   Page: 405
Topic: Three Kinds of Learning—Classical Conditioning

13. Pavlov's experiments on the timing of associations demonstrated that two things become associated because
    a. one concept is simply attached to another concept.
    b. the UCS always precedes the CS.
    c. one concept changes the meaning of the other concept.
    d. physical responses can only be elicited by physical stimuli.

    Answer: c   Page: 406
    Topic: Three Kinds of Learning—Classical Conditioning

14. If the CS fails to be followed by the UCS many times, the organism will experience
    a. extinction.
    b. habituation.
    c. stimulus generalization.
    d. counterconditioning.

    Answer: a   Page: 407
    Topic: Three Kinds of Learning—Classical Conditioning

15. As an adult, Jenny loves rocking chairs. She likes sitting in them, buying them, and just looking at them. Her emotional reaction to rocking chairs is most likely attributable to
    a. second-order conditioning.
    b. habituation.
    c. counterconditioning.
    d. operant conditioning.

    Answer: a   Page: 407
    Topic: Three Kinds of Learning—Classical Conditioning

16. Which of the following cannot be classically conditioned?
    a. Eye blinks
    b. Claustrophobia
    c. Insulin release by the pancreas
    d. None of the above

    Answer: d   Pages: 407–411
    Topic: Three Kinds of Learning—Classical Conditioning

17. It has been suggested that chronic anxiety is the result of
    a. pairing a primary reinforcer with a punisher.
    b. the law of effect.
    c. repeated exposure to stimuli that are unpredictable and random.
    d. second-order conditioning and stimulus generalization.

    Answer: c   Page: 409
    Topic: Three Kinds of Learning—Classical Conditioning

18. Thorndike's Law of Effect is
    a. a response will be strengthened if it is paired with a desirable outcome.
    b. an organism will stop responding if a conditioned stimulus fails to be followed by the unconditioned stimulus.
    c. stimuli that are similar to the conditioned stimulus will elicit the same response.
    d. behaviors that have many effects are more likely to be incorporated into an organism's personality.

    Answer: a   Pages: 411–412
    Topic: Three Kinds of Learning—Operant Conditioning

19. A major difference between the ideas of Hull and Thorndike is, unlike Thorndike, Hull thought that
    a. behavior was a function of events in the environment.
    b. learning should be conceived in terms of stimuli and response linkings.
    c. behavior was a function of the properties of the organism.
    d. the Law of Effect was very similar to classical conditioning.

    Answer: c   Page: 412
    Topic: Three Kinds of Learning—Operant Conditioning

20. Skinner was one of the first to insist that classical conditioning and operant conditioning
    a. function through the same mechanisms.
    b. explain all forms of learning equally well.
    c. are different types of learning.
    d. a and b.

    Answer: c   Page: 413
    Topic: Three Kinds of Learning—Operant Conditioning

21. Behavior that acts on the environment and changes it to the organism's advantage is _____ behavior.
    a. respondent
    b. reinforced
    c. operant
    d. shaping

    Answer: c   Page: 413
    Topic: Three Kinds of Learning—Operant Conditioning

22. A light goes on in a room just before an excruciatingly loud buzzer sounds. A subject who startles when the light goes on shows _____ behavior but one who leaves the room to avoid the noise exhibits _____ behavior.
    a. respondent; operant
    b. operant; respondent

c. conditioned; counterconditioned
d. counterconditioned; conditioned

Answer: a   Page: 413
Topic: Three Kinds of Learning—Operant Conditioning

23. On the first day of kindergarten, Terry's teacher responds to the students
    every time they ask her a question. By the end of the first week, the teacher
    will only respond to students who are sitting quietly at their desks. At the
    end of the second week, the teacher will only respond to students' questions
    if they are quietly seated, raise their hand, and wait to be called on before
    asking their question. Terry's teacher is using _____ to change the
    students' behavior.
    a. habituation
    b. shaping
    c. punishment
    d. secondary conditioning

Answer: b   Pages: 414–415
Topic: Three Kinds of Learning—Operant Conditioning

24. It has been suggested that _____ is better for explaining aspects of
    personality that are behaviorally based while _____ is better for
    explaining those that are emotionally based.
    a. habituation; operant conditioning
    b. classical conditioning; social learning theory
    c. associationism; the Law of Effect
    d. operant conditioning; classical conditioning

Answer: d   Page: 417
Topic: Classical and Operant Conditioning Compared

25. Punishment involves
    a. removing an aversive stimulus in order to increase the frequency of a
       behavior.
    b. introducing an aversive consequence in order to decrease the frequency
       of a behavior.
    c. reinforcing incompatible behavioral responses.
    d. a and b.

Answer: b   Page: 417
Topic: Punishment

26. Perhaps the biggest problem associated with the use of punishment is that
    a. behaviorists have not been able to identify consequences that are
       generally punishing.

b. it is almost always administered incorrectly.

c. alternatives to punishment are seldom available.

d. punishing only the specific behavior does not appear to reduce the frequency of that behavior.

Answer: b   Page: 417
Topic: Punishment

27. It has been suggested the most effective way to decrease the frequency of an undesirable behavior is to

a. reinforce the undesirable behavior.

b. punish the undesirable behavior.

c. reward an incompatible behavior.

d. avoid using secondary punishing stimuli.

Answer: c   Page: 418
Topic: How to Punish

28. One danger associated with the use of punishment is

a. that it is difficult for the punisher to gauge the severity of the punishment.

b. that punishment motivates concealment of behavior and avoidance of the punisher.

c. that punishment teaches about power differentials.

d. all of the above

Answer: d   Pages: 421–423
Topic: Dangers of Punishment

29. A parent who relies heavily on punishment to correct his or her child's behavior is likely to find that the child

a. is well behaved even when the parent is not around.

b. grows up to be an aggressive adult.

c. avoids them whenever possible.

d. b and c.

Answer: d   Pages: 422–423
Topic: Dangers of Punishment

30. Behaviorism's most important intellectual contribution may be its insistence that

a. psychologists should focus on observable behaviors.

b. the conscious mind determines behavior.

c. emotion is the primary motivator of human behavior.

d. human beings have free will

Answer: a   Page: 423
Topic: Contributions and Shortcomings of Behaviorism

31. The idea that in time, you can get used to almost anything is associated with which kind of learning mechanism?
    a. Habituation
    b. Classical conditioning
    c. Operant conditioning
    d. b and c

    Answer: a   Page: 405
    Topic: Three Kinds of Learning—Habituation

32. An advertising executive has created a television ad campaign for a new sports car. The commercial shows a very attractive woman getting into the car and making a comment about how powerful the car seems to be. This ad is (obviously) aimed at men and is intended to elicit a positive feeling about the car. In this commercial, the attractive woman is _____, the car is _____, and the positive feeling about the car is

    _____.
    a. a conditioned stimulus; an unconditioned stimulus; a conditioned response
    b. an unconditioned stimulus; a conditioned stimulus; a conditioned response
    c. an unconditioned response; a conditioned response; a conditioned stimulus
    d. an operant stimulus; a classical stimulus; a habituated stimulus

    Answer: b   Page: 406
    Topic: Basics of Classical Conditioning

CHAPTER 16

Motivation, Thought, and Behavior: The Social Learning Theories

OUTLINE

SUMMARY

Three different social learning theories have been constructed by psychologists trying to extend behaviorism's basic tenets and empirical approach to cover topics that classical behaviorism neglects. Dollard and Miller's social learning theory explains motivation as the result of primary and secondary drives, aggression as the result of frustration, and psychological conflict as the result of the interplay of motivations to approach and avoid a goal. Dollard and Miller also offer a reinforcement-based explanation of some psychoanalytic defense mechanisms.

Rotter's social learning theory offers an explanation of how people make decisions. His expectancy value theory describes an individual's behavioral potential (tendency to do something) as a function of his or her expectancies, the reinforcement value of the goal, and the particular situation. This theory is presented in the form of a quasi-mathematical formula. Rotter also offers an account of psychological maladjustment and prescriptions for psychotherapy.

Bandura's social learning theory includes a notion of efficacy expectations that closely resembles Rotter's expectancies. Bandura's theory goes beyond Rotter's, however, in two important ways. Bandura describes the process of observational learning, in which one learns by watching the behaviors and outcomes of others, and he also describes the process of reciprocal determinism, in which one's actions are determined by a self system that originates in the environment, then changes the environment, which in turn affects the self system.

Learning approaches to personality have epitomized objective research, drawn necessary attention to the importance of the environment, and yielded a useful technology of behavioral change. However, not all behavior changes are long lasting or generalizable, and in general learning approaches underemphasize the importance of complex cognitive processes.

ABOUT THE CHAPTER

Even some psychologists may be surprised to learn—I was—that the well-known theories by Dollard and Miller, by Rotter, and by Bandura were all originally called social learning theory. All three are extensions of behaviorism, although they pursue their extension in somewhat different directions.

The material in this chapter is important, but social learning theory—of any of these three varieties—no longer seems a very active current topic in personality psychology. Most current investigators in this area seem to have moved on to the cognitive social learning or just cognitive approaches such as described in the next chapter.

TEACHING NOTES

Of all the material in this text, I find that included in this chapter to be the most difficult to bring to life for students. Much of it is at a very high level of abstraction and badly needs the apt example and infusion of common sense. My advice to an instructor would simply be to use as many specific examples in lecture as you can come up with.

The pseudo-mathematical formula by Rotter is worth showing to students—it is also included in the selection by Rotter in the reader—but students need to have explained that the formula should not be taken too seriously. It is little more than a shorthand way of describing Rotter's ideas about the causation of behavior. There is a general point to be made here, I think, concerning the use of pseudo-formulas (i.e., formulas into which you cannot actually plug numbers and perform calculations) in psychology.

PIECES OF THE PERSONALITY PUZZLE

The selections in Part VII of the reader by Rotter and Bandura pertain directly to material in this chapter. The Rotter article includes more about his behavioral prediction formula. The Bandura article is his famous original study of learning by imitation in which children ended up bashing a Bobo doll.

DISCUSSION QUESTIONS

1. Do you think it is possible to reconcile psychoanalysis with learning theory, as Dollard and Miller tried to do? Is it a good idea to even try?

2. Have you ever had something in the future that you were both looking forward to and dreading? Did your feelings about it change over time in the way Dollard and Miller describe?

3. Do you think people just want to lash out when they are frustrated, as described by Dollard and Miller's frustration-aggression hypothesis? Can you think of examples that demonstrate this? How about cases where this did *not* happen? What does a person's reaction to frustration depend on?

4. Do you think Rotter's behavioral prediction formula adds anything over and above a verbal statement of the same ideas stated in words? What do you think about efforts to make psychological statements mathematical in this way?

5. Can you think of other ways—beyond those described by Bandura—in which people make their own environments?

6. A person is under severe stress because both at home and at work he seems surrounded by angry people. According to Bandura's analysis, what might be going on?

MULTIPLE-CHOICE QUESTIONS

1. Unlike social learning theory, behaviorism
   a. views human beings as passive organisms.
   b. ignores observational learning.
   c. ignores motivation and cognition.
   d. all of the above.

   Answer: d   Pages: 425–426
   Topic: What Behaviorism Leaves Out

2. Dollard and Miller's key idea concerns
   a. defense mechanisms.
   b. the habit hierarchy.
   c. behavior potential.
   d. reciprocal determinism.

   Answer: b   Page: 427
   Topic: Dollard and Miller's Social Learning Theory

3. A ranked ordering of the behaviors that an individual might do is called
   a. an expectancy value theory.
   b. an efficacy expectation list.
   c. a habit hierarchy.
   d. a behavior potential.

   Answer: c   Page: 427
   Topic: Dollard and Miller's Social Learning Theory

4. Dollard and Miller's social learning theory differs from other social learning
   approaches because it attempts to explain
   a. traditionally Freudian concepts and phenomena.
   b. cognitive processes ignored by behaviorists.
   c. the role of expectancy.
   d. the acquisition of reinforcement values.

   Answer: a   Page: 427
   Topic: Dollard and Miller's Social Learning Theory

5. According to Dollard and Miller, a state of psychological tension that feels
   good when it is reduced is called
   a. a behavior potential.
   b. a drive.

   c. motivation.
   d. psychological conflict.

Answer: b   Page: 428
Topic: Motivation and Drives

6. From Dollard and Miller's perspective on behavior, love, prestige, power, fear, and humiliation are
   a. secondary drives.
   b. primary reinforcers.
   c. primary drives.
   d. biological needs.

Answer: a   Page: 428
Topic: Motivation and Drives

7. According to Dollard and Miller, in order for a reward to be reinforcing and produce behavior change, the reward must
   a. increase the expectancy value of the behavior.
   b. change the habit hierarchy.
   c. satisfy a need.
   d. produce physiological tension.

Answer: c   Page: 429
Topic: Motivation and Drives

8. According to Dollard and Miller, _____ provides the motivating force for human behavior.
   a. expectancy
   b. self-efficacy
   c. reinforcement value
   d. drive reduction

Answer: d   Pages: 428–429
Topic: Motivation and Drives

9. If you are frustrated because your coworker's performance prevented you from getting the end-of-the-year bonus you were expecting, Dollard and Miller would predict that you would respond to this frustration with
   a. depression.
   b. aggressive behavior.
   c. feelings of humiliation.
   d. avoidance of the situation.

Answer: b   Pages: 430–431
Topic: Frustration and Aggression

10. Research on the drive-reduction function of displacement indicates that if you displace your aggression, it will
    a. make you feel frustration.
    b. not necessarily reduce the aggressive drive.
    c. typically reduce the aggressive drive.
    d. none of the above.

    Answer: b   Page: 431
    Topic: Frustration and Aggression

11. As a conflicted goal gets closer, the tendency to _____ goal becomes stronger than the corresponding tendency to _____ goal.
    a. avoid a negative; approach a positive
    b. approach a negative; approach a positive
    c. approach a negative; avoid a positive
    d. avoid a positive; avoid a negative

    Answer: a   Page: 431
    Topic: Psychological Conflict

12. Dollard and Miller view psychological conflict as the result of
    a. conflict between the id and the superego.
    b. conflict between primary and secondary drives.
    c. habit hierarchy disorder.
    d. approach-avoidance conflict.

    Answer: d   Page: 431
    Topic: Psychological Conflict

13. Defense mechanisms, according to Dollard and Miller, are
    a. internal drive states that cause aggression.
    b. affective mechanisms for coping with stress caused by the approach-avoidance conflict.
    c. cognitive behaviors that are negatively reinforced because they remove anxiety.
    d. mechanisms used by the ego to defend against anxiety produced by psychic conflict.

    Answer: c   Page: 433
    Topic: Defense Mechanisms

14. Julian Rotter's social learning theory focuses primarily on
    a. drives.
    b. decision making.

   c. efficacy expectations.

   d. reciprocal determinism.

Answer: b   Page: 434

Topic: Rotter's Social Learning Theory

15. Mark thinks that if he asks for a $50 a week raise, he will definitely get it. He really wants a $75 a week raise and thinks his chances of getting that are about 50-50. Expectancy value theory would predict that Mark will ask for a _____ a week raise and classic behaviorism would predict that he'll ask for a _____ a week raise.

   a. $50; $75

   b. $75; $50

   c. $50; $50

   d. $75; $75

Answer: a   Page: 434

Topic: Expectancy Value Theory of Decision Making

16. From the perspective of expectancy value theory, the probability that you will perform a behavior in a given situation is called your _____, and your belief about how likely a behavior is to attain a certain goal is called your _____.

   a. expectancy; behavior potential

   b. behavior potential; expectancy

   c. reinforcement value; expectancy

   d. efficacy expectation; behavior expectation

Answer: b   Pages: 434–435

Topic: Expectancy Value Theory of Decision Making

17. According to Rotter, locus of control is analogous to

   a. self-efficacy.

   b. a specific expectancy.

   c. reinforcement value.

   d. a generalized expectancy.

Answer: d   Page: 436

Topic: Expectancy Value Theory of Decision Making

18. Being in a relationship is very important to Brian but is only moderately important to Matthew. Brian and Matthew have different _____ for being in a relationship.

   a. expectancies

   b. behavior potentials

c. efficacy expectations
d. reinforcement values

Answer: d   Page: 437
Topic: Expectancy Value Theory of Decision Making

19. One translation of Rotter's formula is $BP_{x, S1, Ra} = f(E_{x, Ra, S1} \& RV_{a, S1})$
    a. behavior is a function of the relative importance of the situation and the psychological environment.
    b. at any given moment, your behavior, personality, and the environment reciprocally determine one another.
    c. what you are likely to do depends on whether you think you can get something and how badly you want it under the circumstances.
    d. behavior problems are a function of efficacy expectations and variability in reinforcement histories.

Answer: c   Page: 438
Topic: Expectancy Value Theory of Decision Making

20. Jake really wants to have a Ph.D. in botany but seriously doubts that he'll be able to finish and defend his dissertation. According to Rotter, Jake
    a. is experiencing low self-efficacy.
    b. has an internal locus of control.
    c. will probably become frustrated and act aggressively.
    d. will likely experience depression.

Answer: d   Pages: 438–439
Topic: Adjustment and Maladjustment

21. In Rotter's expectancy value theory, psychological conflict results from having
    a. two or more behaviors with high RVs.
    b. an internal locus of control.
    c. conflict in approach-avoidance system.
    d. expectancies that are higher than your self-efficacy.

Answer: a   Page: 439
Topic: Adjustment and Maladjustment

22. Rotterian psychotherapy focuses on
    a. drive reduction.
    b. goal and expectancy clarification.
    c. resolving approach-avoidance conflict.
    d. changing efficacy expectations.

Answer: b   Page: 440
Topic: Psychotherapy

23. Bandura's concept of efficacy is similar to what Rotter called
    a. situational relativism.
    b. reinforcement values.
    c. expectancies.
    d. behavior potential.

    Answer: c   Page: 441
    Topic: Efficacy Expectations

24. Barbara thinks that Joe will go out on a date with her *if* she can ever get up
    the courage to ask him. Barbara's perception of the likelihood that Joe will
    accept reflects her _____, while her doubts about her ability to ask
    him out reflect her _____.
    a. reinforcement value; behavior potential
    b. expectancy; efficacy expectation
    c. efficacy expectation; expectancy
    d. behavior potential; reinforcement value

    Answer: b   Page: 441
    Topic: Efficacy Expectations

25. Bandura's efficacy expectation is a belief about
    a. what the person is capable of doing.
    b. what the likely result of a behavior will be.
    c. the worth of an outcome.
    d. all of the above.

    Answer: a   Page: 441
    Topic: Efficacy Expectations

26. The key target for psychotherapy, according to Bandura, is to
    a. change the client's overt behavior.
    b. achieve a match between the client's efficacies and capabilities.
    c. change the client's reinforcement values.
    d. modify the client's habit hierarchy.

    Answer: b   Page: 441
    Topic: Efficacy Expectations

27. The Bobo doll studies of aggression demonstrated that
    a. changing efficacy expectations can facilitate behavioral change.
    b. expectancies vary across situations.
    c. children will imitate positive but not negative behaviors.
    d. learning can occur vicariously through observation.

    Answer: d   Page: 444
    Topic: Observational Learning

28. The element of reciprocal determinism that is the most significant departure from classic behaviorism is the idea that
    a. the organism's behavior is a function of the environment.
    b. the environment cannot be changed by an organism's behavior.
    c. the self can affect behavior independently of the environment.
    d. learning occurs through direct reinforcement for behavior.

    Answer: c   Page: 446
    Topic: Reciprocal Determinism and the Self

29. As a child, Robin was frequently surrounded by many people and came to see herself as a very sociable person. As an adult, Robin has chosen a career that requires her to interact with other people on a daily basis and, as a result, is becoming even more sociable than before. This process is called
    a. the approach-avoidance goal system.
    b. reciprocal determinism.
    c. vicarious learning.
    d. the expectancy value theory.

    Answer: b   Pages: 445–446
    Topic: Reciprocal Determinism and the Self

30. All of the social learning theorists discussed in the text agree that the important causes of behavior
    a. are located in the environment.
    b. involve an interaction between the individual's mind and the environment.
    c. are located in the conscious mind.
    d. result from direct reinforcement for the behavior.

    Answer: b   Page: 446
    Topic: Reciprocal Determinism and the Self

31. Whereas classic behaviorism states that learning affects behavior, Dollard and Miller's social theory of learning states that learning affects
    a. the association between a UCS and a CR.
    b. the hierarchy of behaviors that an organism might do.
    c. an organism's self-system.
    d. a and b.

    Answer: b   Page: 427
    Topic: Dollard and Miller's Social Learning Theory

32. From Bandura's perspective, if you are faced with a threat and you have low self-efficacy about your ability to cope with it, then you will experience _____; if you have a great desire to obtain something but you have

low self-efficacy about your ability to obtain it, then you will experience
_____.
a. anxiety; depression
b. depression; anxiety
c. angst; displacement
d. angst; habituation

Answer: a   Page: 443
Topic: Bandura's Social Learning Theory

33. The most fundamental limitation of the learning approaches is that they
    a. focus only on psychological disorders and ignore humankind's positive qualities.
    b. underemphasize or ignore cognition.
    c. underemphasize the effect of the specific situation on an organism's behavior.
    d. a and b.

Answer: b   Page: 448
Topic: Contributions and Limitations of the Learning Approaches

34. A major achievement of the learning approaches to personality psychology is that they
    a. pushed psychology in the direction of an objective science.
    b. enhanced our understanding of how the environment affects behavior.
    c. led to the development of useful procedures for changing behavior.
    d. all of the above.

Answer: d   Pages: 446–447
Topic: Contributions and Limitations of the Learning Approaches

CHAPTER 17	The Cognitive System and the Personality System

OUTLINE

SUMMARY

An important, relatively new area of research draws connections between personality functioning and the processes of perception and memory long studied by cognitive psychology. This new research derived from social learning theory (which itself derived from behaviorism), and also is influenced by phenomenological theorists such as George Kelly. A serial view of the cognitive system views mental functioning as consisting of the flow of information through a sensory buffer into short-term memory, working memory, and in some cases into long-term memory. The concept of the sensory buffer implies that personality may affect what information is perceived, and short-term memory implies a limit to phenomenological consciousness. The distinction between declarative and procedural memory in long-term memory implies that we might sometimes know something—such as what it means to feel an emotion—without being able to describe it. A more recent, parallel (PDP) view of the cognitive system views it as made up of many different systems operating simultaneously. This view is compatible with the psychoanalytic idea of thought and behavior as representing a compromise among competing mental subsystems, as well as with Walter Mischel's modern Cognitive-Affective Personality System (CAPS) theory of personality. Mischel's theory identifies five cognitive person variables that are important for understanding personality and behavior. Seymour Epstein's Cognitive-Experiential Self-theory (CEST) describes the parallel operations of experiential and rational systems of thought. The first, evolutionary older system, operates outside of conscious awareness and is particularly relevant to emotion, intuition, and wisdom. The second, uniquely human system is conscious, logical, and rational.

ABOUT THE CHAPTER

This chapter begins by tracing how cognitive approaches developed out of social learning theory (especially Bandura's version), which developed from behaviorism. Next, a generic serial model of how the mind processes information is presented. Along the way, I try to point out where aspects of information processing the model are relevant to personality processes. Then, new to the Second Edition, I consider the parallel processing approach to cognition and its implications for personality. Finally, the chapter presents two modern cognitive perspectives on personality, by Mischel and by Epstein. Both are new to this edition. The discussion of Mischel's CAPS system is updated from his cognitive social learning approach from which it developed recently. The presence of a major section on Epstein's cognitive-experiential self-theory may surprise some instructors. Epstein isn't ordinarily considered a social-cognitive theorist, but his approach is an interesting attempt to integrate cognition and psychoanalysis and can be used to generate many vivid examples for class lectures and discussion.

TEACHING NOTES

Although the cognitive approach to personality now deserves to be considered as a new and separate paradigm, it derived closely from social learning theory which itself derived from behaviorism. I think it is important to explain this lineage to students because it accounts for certain aspects of the cognitive approach that otherwise would seem paradoxical (e.g., the reluctance of some theorists to acknowledge the existence of behavioral consistency). An instructor can note that the two best-known cognitive theorists of personality—Bandura and Mischel— were previously among the important developers of social learning theory.

Many students will find this material dry. I recommend the generous use of examples. The abstract cognitive principles are best learned through examples of the cocktail party effect, or the feeling of having many different thoughts and perceptions going on at once or the contrast between knowing rationally what to do and what one feels like doing (Epstein). An instructor familiar with the current literature in cognitive psychology could draw on it for lecture material.

PIECES OF THE PERSONALITY PUZZLE

For this chapter the articles in Part VIII by Bandura, Mischel, and Epstein are directly relevant.

DISCUSSION QUESTIONS

1. Have you taken a course in cognitive psychology? If so, do you think that approach can be integrated into personality psychology?

2. Have you ever heard something but not really heard it (e.g., the cocktail party effect)? What was this like? What were the consequences?

3. What is thinking? Is it an orderly sequential process or is it more like a complex buzzing of many different things going on at the same time?

4. Are people different from each other because they think differently? Are there other ways in which one individual's personality can differ from that of another ?

5. Have you ever thought one thing was the right thing to do but felt like doing something else? Was this because, as Epstein says, your rational system and your emotional system have different goals?

MULTIPLE-CHOICE QUESTIONS

1. Which of the following has influenced the cognitive approach to personality?
   a. Phenomenological approach
   b. Behaviorism
   c. Psychoanalysis
   d. All of the above

   Answer: d   Pages: 455–456
   Topic: Roots of the Cognitive Approach

2. The view of the mind as _____ suggests that the mind functions in distinct and ordered steps. The view of the mind as _____ suggests that many different processes operate in the mind all at once.
   a. a parallel system; a serial system
   b. a serial system; a parallel system
   c. a conscious unit; an unconscious unit
   d. a cognitive system; a personality system

   Answer: b   Page: 457
   Topic: The Cognitive System

3. The sensory-perceptual buffer, short-term memory, working memory, and long-term memory all fall within a view of the mind as _____.
   a. a serial system
   b. a parallel system
   c. a schematic system
   d. none of the above

   Answer: a   Page: 458
   Topic: The Serial System

4. The sensory-perceptual buffer can only hold
   a. about seven chunks of information.
   b. information for less than two or three seconds.
   c. visual information while the original stimulus is still present.
   d. information that has been identified and interpreted by the perceiver.

   Answer: b   Page: 458
   Topic: The Sensory-Perceptual Buffer

5. Research on the cocktail party effect demonstrates that
   a. between five and nine pieces of information can be held in short-term memory.

b. alcohol consumption interferes with the information transfer between working memory and long-term memory.

c. information that enters our sensory-perceptual buffer outside of our conscious awareness is being monitored and can be retrieved.

d. ego defense mechanisms may prevent certain anxiety-provoking stimuli from entering consciousness.

Answer: c   Pages: 459–460
Topic: The Sensory-Perceptual Buffer

6. The selective functioning of the sensory-perceptual buffer has been tentatively linked to the psychoanalytic concept of
a. defense mechanisms.
b. parapraxes.
c. the preconscious mind.
d. sublimation.

Answer: a   Page: 460
Topic: The Sensory-Perceptual Buffer

7. The phrase "seven plus or minus two" refers to the
a. number of seconds information can be held in the perceptual buffer.
b. capacity of short-term memory.
c. number of years information can be stored in long-term memory before it is replaced with new information.
d. organizational structure of schemas.

Answer: b   Page: 461
Topic: Short-Term Memory

8. According to research on short-term memory, which of the following could be easily retained in short-term memory?
a. Twelve single digit numbers (e.g., 1, 9, 6, 2, 4, 2, 5, 9, 3, 0, 7, 7)
b. Ten first names
c. Six phone numbers including area codes
d. The names of twenty unrelated but commonly used household products

Answer: c   Page: 461
Topic: Short-Term Memory

9. Short-term memory is roughly equivalent to _____ thought and working memory is similar to _____ thought.
a. unconscious; subconscious
b. preconscious; unconscious

c. subconscious; conscious
d. conscious; preconscious

Answer: d   Pages: 462–463
Topic: Short-Term Memory

10. As a person becomes an expert in an area, he or she will begin to
_____ to help organize the information.
a. use larger chunks
b. develop incremental theories
c. use smaller chunks
d. a and b

Answer: a   Page: 462
Topic: Short-Term Memory

11. This morning you noticed that you needed some things from the grocery
store. While at the store, you will use _____ memory to recall
those items into consciousness.
a. declarative
b. procedural
c. working
d. short-term

Answer: c   Page: 463
Topic: Working Memory

12. Research indicates that the most effective way to commit information to
long-term memory is
a. to repeat the information over and over again.
b. to limit your attention to about seven specific pieces of information.
c. to ask yourself, "How does this information apply to me?"
d. all of the above.

Answer: c   Page: 464
Topic: From Short-Term to Long-Term Memory

13. The consensus of modern cognitive psychologists is that the storage
capacity of long-term memory is
a. essentially limitless.
b. limited to about seven chunks of information.
c. decreases with age.
d. increases with age.

Answer: a   Pages: 464–465
Topic: Long-Term Memory

14. If you know that Freud used the technique of free association in psychotherapy you have _____ about free association. If you know how to use the technique of free association yourself, you have _____.
    a. long-term storage; working memory
    b. perceptual knowledge; sensory knowledge
    c. declarative knowledge; procedural knowledge
    d. event memory; conceptual memory

    Answer: c   Pages: 465–470
    Topic: Long-Term Memory

15. _____ memory contains your general knowledge of the world and an understanding of how it works.
    a. Conceptual
    b. Event
    c. Procedural
    d. Working

    Answer: a   Page: 466
    Topic: Long-Term Memory

16. Your expectations about sequences of events that should occur in certain situations are called cognitive
    a. schemas.
    b. expectancies.
    c. scripts.
    d. heuristics.

    Answer: c   Page: 466
    Topic: Long-Term Memory

17. On Jason's first visit to a psychologist, he was surprised to find that his psychologist did not resemble Freud in either looks or behavior and didn't ask him to lay on a couch and recite his dreams. Jason's trip to the psychologist did not match his _____ about psychologists and therapy sessions.
    a. cognitive and behavioral constructions
    b. procedural and declarative knowledge
    c. encoding strategies and personal constructs
    d. stereotypes and scripts

    Answer: d   Pages: 466–467
    Topic: Long-Term Memory

18. Knowing how to swim, act charming, and tell a joke are generally learned by acquiring _____ knowledge.
    a. conceptual
    b. procedural
    c. declarative
    d. event

    Answer: b   Page: 468
    Topic: Long-Term Memory

19. Your art teacher is trying to help you improve your painting techniques. She encourages you to just choose a subject and begin painting and later gives you feedback on your completed painting. Your art teacher is attempting to teach
    a. subjective stimulus values.
    b. procedural knowledge.
    c. encoding strategies.
    d. construction competencies.

    Answer: b   Pages: 468–469
    Topic: Long-Term Memory

20. Emotions are a separate category of
    a. encoding strategies.
    b. subjective stimulus values.
    c. procedural knowledge.
    d. declarative memories.

    Answer: c   Page: 469
    Topic: Long-Term Memory

21. Which of the following is a reason that dissatisfaction has arisen with the serial way of describing the cognitive system?
    a. The serial model seems incompatible with what is known about the architecture of the brain.
    b. The serial model seems like it would be too slow to perform many normal cognitive and perceptual tasks.
    c. The serial model seems incompatible with many known personality functions.
    d. a and b.

    Answer: d   Page: 470
    Topic: Limitations of the Serial Model

22. Which of the following is not an implication of the PDP view of the cognitive system?
    a. It explains why perception happens so fast and feels immediate.
    b. Whichever receivers are most active will tend to respond most quickly.
    c. Computers are a poor models for personality processes
    d. The result of cognitive activity is a compromise among many different processes.

    Answer: c   Pages: 472–473
    Topic: The Parallel System

23. In his theory of the Cognitive-Affective Personality System, Mischel suggests that the most important aspect of the different systems of personality and cognition is
    a. their influence on personality traits.
    b. the way in which they simultaneously interact.
    c. the reciprocal determinism between thought and behavior.
    d. that they create an approach to personality that integrates the trait and cognitive perspectives.

    Answer: b   Page: 474
    Topic: The Cognitive-Affective Personality System

24. Which of the following theorists is most closely associated with the idea that personality is a stable system that mediates how the individual collects, construes, and processes social information and generates social behaviors?
    a. Sigmund Freud
    b. B. F. Skinner
    c. Walter Mischel
    d. Seymour Epstein

    Answer: c   Page: 474
    Topic: The Cognitive-Affective Personality System

25. According to Mischel, _____ comprise a person's intelligence, social skills, and creativity.
    a. encoding strategies and personal constructs
    b. subjective stimulus values
    c. self-regulatory systems
    d. cognitive and behavioral construction competencies

    Answer: d   Page: 475
    Topic: Cognitive Person Variables

26. In Mischel's theory, the person variables of _____ correspond to Bandura's self system and _____ correspond to Rotter's notion of expectancies.

a. self-regulatory systems and plans; subjective stimulus values
b. encoding strategies and personal constructs; subjective stimulus values
c. behavioral construction competencies; cognitive competencies
d. personal constructs; plans

Answer: a   Page: 475
Topic: Cognitive Person Variables

27. The person variables in Mischel's CAPS theory that include procedures for the control of one's behavior and thoughts are the
a. encoding strategies and personal constructs
b. subjective stimulus values
c. self-regulatory systems
d. cognitive and behavioral construction competencies

Answer: c   Page: 475
Topic: Cognitive Person Variables

28. Whereas Michel's CAPS theory of personality emphasizes _____, Epstein's CEST theory emphasizes _____.
a. unconscious processing and the seemingly irrational, emotion-driven sectors of the mind; conscious experience, phenomenology, and rational thought
b. conscious experience, phenomenology, and rational thought; unconscious processing and the seemingly irrational, emotion-driven sectors of the mind
c. personality traits; cognitive person variables
d. a and c

Answer: b   Page: 476
Topic: Cognitive-Experiential Self Theory

29. In Epstein's Cognitive-Experiential Self Theory, the _____ system dominates when you are emotional and the _____ system dominates when you are calm.
a. cognitive; experiential
b. experiential; cognitive
c. experiential; rational
d. self; cognitive

Answer: b   Page: 477
Topic: Cognitive-Experiential Self Theory

30. Which of the following is not characteristic of the experiential system?
a. It operates at high speed.
b. It operates outside of consciousness.

c. Its knowledge can be gained only through experience.
d. It operates without emotion.

Answer: d   Pages: 476–478
Topic: Cognitive-Experiential Self Theory

31. Which of the following is a characteristic of the rational system?
    a. It operates through logic.
    b. It operates through emotion, insight and wisdom.
    c. It operates through primarily unconscious processes.
    d. All of the above.

Answer: a   Pages: 476–478
Topic: Cognitive-Experiential Self Theory

32. Jeff has decided to go on a diet and has vowed to avoid desserts. Unfortu-
    nately for Jeff, his mother made her famous pumpkin pie—Jeff's favorite—
    during the Thanksgiving break. After a big dinner, his mother brings out
    the pie and Jeff can't resist having two pieces. In Epstein's terminology,
    Jeff's _____ won out over his _____.
    a. subjective stimulus values; self-regulatory systems
    b. affective system; cognitive system
    c. experiential system; rational system
    d. phenomenology; consciousness

Answer: c   Page: 477
Topic: Cognitive-Experiential Self Theory

CHAPTER 18 | Cognitive Processes and Personality

OUTLINE

I. Perceptual Processes
   A. Priming and Chronic Accessibility
   B. Aggression
   C. Rejection Sensitivity
II. Self Processes
   A. The Self Schema
   B. Consequences of the Self Schema
   C. Many Selves or Just One?
III. Organizational Processes
   A. Strategies
      1. Narrow strategies
      2. Broad strategies
      3. Strategic consistency
   B. Goals
      1. Goals and motivation
      2. Types of goals
         a. General and specific goals
         b. Idiographic and nomothetic goals
            1. Idiographic goals
               a. Current concerns
               b. Personal projects
               c. Personal strivings
               d. Properties and limitations of idiographic goals
            2. Nomothetic goals
               a. The Big Three, or Five, or Two
               b. Judgment goals and development goals
                  1. Entity and incremental theories

SUMMARY

Several cognitive processes are important for personality. *Perceptual processes,* such as priming, affect what we notice in the environment and how we respond to it. Concepts that are chronically accessible are those that are consistently primed within an individual, and this kind of chronic accessibility can influence behavioral patterns such as aggressiveness and rejection sensitivity. *Self processes* guide perception, thought, behavior, and emotion by organizing them around a person's knowledge of who he or she is and what he or she is capable of. People will more readily process information that is relevant to their self schemas, and their emotional states such as depression and anxiety may depend on how their actual self schema contrasts with their images of who they would like to be or think they ought to be. Some theorists maintain that people have many different self schemas used in different contexts; others contest this idea. *Organizational processes* serve to give coherence to many different cognitive and behavioral phenomena. Strategies are sequences of thought and behavior in the service of goals.

Goals are desired end states that serve to motivate thought and behavior. Goals can be hierarchically arranged and can be conceived of in terms of current concerns, personal projects, life tasks, or personal strivings. At a broader level, theorists have proposed that a small number of basic goals are particularly important. Dweck's cognitive approach to motivation distinguishes between two kinds of goals, judgment goals and development goals. These goals derive from the implicit theories people hold. People with judgment goals are entity theorists who believe personality attributes and abilities are fixed and respond to failure with helplessness. People with development goals are incremental theorists who believe attributes and abilities can be changed and respond to failure with even greater effort. In the final analysis, the cognitive approach is more similar to than different from the trait approach. Even though they use somewhat different terminology, both approaches try to describe patterns of individual differences in behavior and the psychological processes behind them.

ABOUT THE CHAPTER

This chapter is mostly new to the Second Edition. It divides the cognitive approaches relevant to personality into three categories (perceptual, self, and organizational processes). Organizational processes include strategies and goals. All of these processes have been addressed by recent research. The chapter concludes with an argument for cognitive approaches to be integrated with, rather than continuing to oppose, the trait approach.

An interesting theme that emerges is the tension between construing processes and individual differences broadly or narrowly. Because of the behaviorist history of the cognitive approach, cognitive theorists often see their variables as relevant only to a narrow range of contexts. This is ironic because one of the most promising directions for developing the cognitive approach is to unify with trait theory to account for the unity of personality.

TEACHING NOTES

As always, this otherwise dry material needs specific examples in order to be successfully communicated. The current state of the cognitive approach to personality is rather disorganized, as befits a relatively new paradigm. This can make it difficult to teach in any well-structured manner. The framework I use—perceptual, self, and organizational processes—is not standard to the field (I'm not aware of anyone else who uses it) but may serve at least for teaching purposes and perhaps be more generally useful as well.

Students new to psychology are often confused by disputes among psychologists, and also can easily draw the impression that psychology is a useless field where nobody agrees about anything. So I recommend instructors ignore the way many social-cognitive writers go out of their way to pick fights with the trait theorists. Instead, one can teach the cognitive approach in a positive way, focusing on the topics that it clarifies and the ways in which it might be usefully integrated with the trait approach.

A theme to emphasize here is that the increased integration across subfields of psychology is a salutary development and the interface of cognitive and personality psychology is one important example. In my experience, students dislike what they perceive as the disorganized nature of personality psychology—so many paradigms! A lecture on the prospects for integrating the cognitive and trait approaches might allow the course to end on a positive, integrative note.

PIECES OF THE PERSONALITY PUZZLE

Part VIII of the reader has articles by Norem, Lyubomirsky et al., and Klein et al. that are directly relevant. Norem's work (with Cantor) is summarized in this chapter. The Klein article, which is also summarized here, is particularly interesting in that it integrates not just cognitive and trait perspectives but also neurobiology. The research by Lyubomirsky is not summarized in this chapter, but her article in the reader is relevant to its themes. One can also look back to the McCrae and Costa article in Part II of the reader, which presents an account of the workings of the Big Five that is not at all incompatible with the cognitive approach. What they call characteristic adaptations overlap with what cognitive theorists call strategies, goals, and implicit theories.

DISCUSSION QUESTIONS

1. What do you find more useful for thinking about people: personality trait concepts or concepts such as strategies and plans? Does the preferred concept depend on your purpose?

2. You surely act in different ways with different people in different situations. Does this mean you have more than one self? Or is there a single self that integrates what you do across situations even though your behavior varies?

3. Do you think optimistic and pessimistic strategies work equally well in motivating academic performance? What are some advantages and disadvantages of each strategy? Which one do you use?

4. Do you know any entity or incremental theorists, as described by Dweck? How do they act? What do they do after they fail at something? What do they do after they succeed?

5. What ideas from other approaches can you find in the cognitive approach to personality? Do you think it will someday absorb these other approaches?

MULTIPLE-CHOICE QUESTIONS

1. Which of the following is a way in which our thoughts influence our actions and our personalities?
   a. The way we perceive and interpret the world
   b. The way we regard ourselves
   c. The way we set goals and make plans to achieve those goals
   d. All of the above

   Answer: d   Page: 481
   Topic: Cognitive Processes and Personality

2. The core idea behind the mechanism of priming is
   a. the more often one perceives something or thinks about it, the more likely that thing will come to mind.
   b. the more unique an object or event is, the more likely it will come to mind.

c. human beings are biologically predisposed to develop phobias of certain objects like snakes and spiders.

d. none of the above.

Answer: a   Page: 482
Topic: Priming and Chronic Accessibility

3. Amy is a generally aggressive and hostile child, and Suzanne just bumped into her in a crowded assembly room. Our knowledge of priming and chronic accessibility would predict that Amy would perceive Suzanne's bump as _____ and that she would be likely to respond with _____.

a. an accident; aggression

b. an accident; an apology

c. an intentionally hostile act; aggression

d. an intentionally hostile act; an apology

Answer: c   Pages: 483–484
Topic: Priming and Chronic Accessibility

4. The cognitive structure that is made up of ideas about yourself that are organized into a coherent whole is your

a. self-efficacy.

b. self regulatory system.

c. personal construct.

d. self schema.

Answer: d   Page: 486
Topic: The Self Schema

5. Paul thinks that he is very intelligent and is aware of the various ways he has demonstrated his intelligence in numerous situations. He interprets his every action and every situation he enters in terms of its relevance to his intelligence. Paul has

a. a cognitive script for intelligence.

b. an elaborate self schema for intelligence.

c. constructed an intelligent possible self.

d. selected intelligence as his current concern.

Answer: b   Pages: 487–488
Topic: The Self Schema

6. According to theories of self-schema, a person can change his or her self-schema by

a. experiencing a serious trauma.

b. imagining a possible self to strive for.

c. experiencing doubt about the world.

d. all of the above.

Answer: d   Page: 487
Topic: The Self Schema

7. His whole life, Tom has been uncomfortable around most other people and has had few friends. All in all, Tom sees himself as very shy, unpopular, and lacking in social skill. Tom was walking across campus yesterday and passed by Arnie, a classmate with whom Tom had worked on a time-consuming project. Arnie did not say hi to Tom or acknowledge him in any way. On the basis of our knowledge of self schemas, we would predict that Tom would

a. interpret Arnie's behavior as indicating that Arnie did not like him.

b. interpret Arnie's behavior as an accident.

c. believe that Arnie himself felt shy and unpopular.

d. feel hostility towards Arnie.

Answer: a   Pages: 487–488
Topic: The Self-Schema

8. From the perspective of self-discrepancy theory, a discrepancy between your actual self and your ideal self results in _____, whereas a discrepancy between your actual self and your ought self results in

_____.

a. disappointment; fear

b. depression; anxiety

c. hostility; punishment

d. a and b

Answer: d   Pages: 488–489
Topic: Consequences of the Self Schema

9. In class you viewed yourself as a student. Now that you have left class and met your friends for lunch, you see yourself as a friend. Your view of yourself as a friend has become your

a. actual self.

b. ideal self.

c. working self-concept.

d. personality contsrual.

Answer: c   Page: 489
Topic: Many Selves or Just One?

10. Bandura has criticized the work on multiple selves on what grounds?

a. Existing theories have not identified a representative range of selves.

b. Once you start fractionating the self, there is no clear place to stop.

c. The concept of a self is unnecessary, since we should concentrate on observable behavior.
d. None of the above.

Answer: b   Pages: 489–490
Topic: Many Selves or Just One?

11. Two kinds of processes have been proposed to explain the organization of the diverse cognitive activities and to maintain coherent patterns of behavior. A _____ is a desired end-state that serves to direct perception, thought, and behavior, and a _____ is an organized sequence of activity in the pursuit of a particular end-state.
a. goal; strategy
b. strategy; goal
c. self-concept; self schema
d. motivation; need

Answer: a   Page: 490
Topic: Organization Processes

12. Josh is discussing what he wants to do after he graduates from college in two years. He tells his parents that he wants to get a job on Wall Street working for a top investment banking firm, to own a BMW, and to make well over $100,000 a year. His parents say, "Well that's fine, Josh, but how do you think you'll accomplish all that? You haven't decided on a major, your grades are barely at a C level, and you've never taken a business or economics class." From the cognitive perspective on personality and behavior, it appears that Josh has not formulated
a. a goal.
b. a strategy.
c. a student concept.
d. a and b.

Answer: b   Page: 490
Topic: Organizational Processes

13. John's parents ask him what he wants to do when he graduates from college in two years. John says, "Well, I'm taking a psychology class, an accounting class, an art class, a history class, and calculus, but I just can't seem to get into anything. I'm not sure what I want to major in, and all these classes I've taken don't seem to lead anywhere. So I certainly don't know what I want to do when I graduate." From the cognitive perspective on personality and behavior, it appears that Josh has not formulated
a. a goal.
b. a strategy.

    c. a student concept.

    d. a and b.

Answer: d   Page: 490

Topic: Organizational Processes

14. Laura attends church regularly because she finds personal meaning and spiritual fulfillment in the rituals and the discussions. Jeanne attends church regularly because she knows that many of the influential business leaders in the community also attend the church, and she wants to take every opportunity to meet them and to make useful contacts. Laura and Jeanne have

    a. the same goals leading to different behaviors.

    b. the same goals leading to the same behavior.

    c. different goals leading to different behaviors.

    d. different goals leading to the same behavior.

Answer: d   Page: 492

Topic: Organizational Processes

15. Research by Julie Norem indicates that defensive pessimists and eternal optimists likely

    a. use different strategies but obtain similar ends.

    b. have similar specific goals but different general goals.

    c. use the same strategies but obtain different ends.

    d. have different learning goals but similar performance goals.

Answer: a   Page: 493

Topic: Strategies

16. I'm preparing for a test in psychology and I tell you that "I'm sure that I'm going to fail. I'm going to study all night, and I'll just be happy with anything higher than a C." You are preparing for the same test and you say, "Oh, come on, we've been going to lecture and keeping up with the reading— we just need to review everything tonight and I'm sure we'll do well on the test." Research on pessimistic and optimistic strategies would predict

    a. that I will get a higher grade on the test than you will.

    b. that you will get a higher grade on the test than I will.

    c. that we will get about the same grade.

    d. none of the above.

Answer: c   Page: 493

Topic: Broad Strategies

17. When asked about consistency in the use of strategies across domains (such as social and academic), cognitive researchers in personality typically insist

a. that there is little or no consistency across domains.
b. that each domain is typically handled with a different strategy.
c. that there is substantial consistency across domains.
d. a and b

Answer: d   Page: 494
Topic: Strategic Consistency

18. General goals serve
    a. to motivate specific behaviors.
    b. to organize daily activities.
    c. to provide a clear purpose in life.
    d. all of the above.

    Answer: d   Pages: 495–496
    Topic: Types of Goals

19. One view of goals is that it is most advantageous to have the ability to
    a. focus primarily on general, long-term goals.
    b. shift between short- and long-term goals.
    c. focus primarily on very specific goals.
    d. set general goals that are separate from your daily activities.

    Answer: b   Page: 496
    Topic: Types of Goals

20. Goals that are unique to the individuals who are pursuing them are
    _____, and goals that organize a wide range of the behavior
    of many people are _____.
    a. strategic goals; motivational goals
    b. judgment goals; developmental goals
    c. nomothetic goals; idiographic goals
    d. idiographic goals; nomothetic goals

    Answer: d   Page: 496
    Topic: Types of Goals

21. Which of the following is not a conceptualization of idiographic goals?
    a. Current concerns
    b. Personal projects
    c. Developmental goals
    d. Personal strivings

    Answer: c   Page: 497
    Topic: Idiographic Goals

22. Idiographic goals share what in common with each other?
    a. They are conscious at least some of the time.
    b. They are assumed to be changeable over time.
    c. They are assumed to be independent of each other.
    d. All of the above.

    Answer: d   Page: 498
    Topic: Idiographic Goals

23. Mrs. Garcia often invites her friends to her house for lunches and parties. She likes to visit her own family as much as she can, and she's very involved with the people in her church group and in the Parent-Teacher Association at her child's school. According to McClelland's view of motivations, Mrs. Garcia is high in
    a. achievement motivation.
    b. affiliation motivation.
    c. power motivation.
    d. all of the above.

    Answer: b   Page: 499
    Topic: Nomothetic Goals

24. Mrs. Khoury enjoys running the office. She likes being able to tell other employees what to work on, when to work on it, and when to stop. She is working hard to be promoted to the level of vice-president on the company. According to McClelland's view of motivations, Mrs. Khoury is high in
    a. achievement motivation.
    b. affiliation motivation.
    c. power motivation.
    d. all of the above.

    Answer: c   Page: 499
    Topic: Nomothetic Goals

25. A _____ goal is one in which an individual is interested in improving himself or herself, and a _____ goal is one in which an individual is seeking to validate an attribute of himself or herself.
    a. general; specific
    b. judgment; development
    c. specific; general
    d. development; judgment

    Answer: d   Page: 500
    Topic: Judgment Goals and Developmental Goals

26. A person with an incremental theory of ability will respond to failure with _____ pattern of behavior.
    a. a helpless

b. a mastery-oriented

c. an anxiety-driven

d. a defensively pessimistic

Answer: b   Pages: 500–501

Topic: Judgment Goals and Developmental Goals

27. A person with an entity theory of ability will respond to failure with
_____ pattern of behavior.

a. a helpless

b. a mastery-oriented

c. an anxiety-driven

d. a defensively pessimistic

Answer: a   Pages: 500–501

Topic: Judgment Goals and Developmental Goals

28. Sharon believes that intelligence and ability are something that you are
just born with and you can't do anything to change them. Sharon has
_____ theory of ability.

a. an entity

b. an incremental

c. a schematic

d. a cognitive

Answer: a   Page: 501

Topic: Judgment Goals and Developmental Goals

29. Steven believes that intelligence and ability can change over time and with
experience. Steven has _____ theory of ability.

a. an entity

b. an incremental

c. a schematic

d. a cognitive

Answer: b   Page: 502

Topic: Judgment Goals and Developmental Goals

30. Which of the following is a similarity between the cognitive approach and
the modern trait approach to personality?

a. Both attempt to identify processes that create individual differences in
behavior.

b. Both attempt to identify the genetic and experiential origins of
individual differences.

c. a and b.

d. None of the above.

Answer: c   Pages: 505–506

Topic: The Cognitive Approach and Its Intersections

Looking Back and Looking Ahead

OUTLINE

SUMMARY

Each of the different approaches to personality psychology has aspects of the person it explains rather well and other aspects it does not explain or ignores entirely. Thus, the choice between them depends not on which one is right but on what one wishes to know. To make progress as a personality psychologist, it is probably necessary to choose one of these approaches, but one should try to stay open to alternative approaches when necessary. In the long run, the various approaches to personality may become increasingly integrated with each other. In the shorter term, the future of personality psychology may include further development of the cognitive approach, renewed attention to emotion and experience, progress in biology and better understanding how biological factors interact with experience, a reconceptualization of cross-cultural approaches, and an increased integration of personality, social, and cognitive psychology. Personality psychology is an attempt to turn our observations of each other into mutual understanding.

ABOUT THE CHAPTER

This chapter provides a brief overview of the principal approaches to personality covered in the preceding chapters. It reiterates what I think is the main point of the book, that the different approaches are not different answers to the same question but to different questions. I consider the prospects for integrating the approaches. I make a case that it is often if not always better to keep these approaches and their questions separate than to mush them together and reveal my own true colors as a trait theorist. It is unlikely any reader will be surprised.

The conclusion I reach concerning the possibility of integration is more optimistic here than it was in the First Edition. I believe that the first hints of how the different strands of personality psychology might be brought together are beginning to appear in the literature.

TEACHING NOTES

Now is the time for an instructor to make all those overview and comparative comments that he or she was tempted to provide to students on the first day of the term. If you have a favorite approach, this is a good time to make a pitch for it. If you disagree with my organization or definition of the basic approaches, this is a good time to explain your own preferred system to your students. In general, this is a good time to come clean about your own biases. I reveal that I am a trait theorist. I would urge an instructor to reveal his or her own favorite approach to students and to explain why it is.

This point in the course also offers one last chance to convince students that personality psychology is meaningful and important. Consider this: Soon, your students will be voting for college construction bonds and representatives who determine the budgets of agencies that award research grants. What do you want them to think about psychology?

DISCUSSION QUESTIONS

1. Is personality psychology really a science? Does the answer to this question matter?

2. What is your favorite approach to personality of those covered? What is your least-favorite approach? Why?

3. Do you think the different approaches to personality will someday be combined into one integrated approach? Should they be?

4. Is personality psychology relevant to the following?
   a. Your own daily life
   b. Understanding and solving social problems
   c. Understanding human nature

5. What do we know when we know a person?

MULTIPLE-CHOICE QUESTIONS

1. The _____ approach focuses on our moment to moment conscious experience, free will, and ability to choose reality.
   a. trait
   b. cognitive
   c. humanistic
   d. all of the above

   Answer: c   Page: 508
   Topic: The Different Approaches

2. Each personality paradigm effectively addresses its own key concerns
   a. and has corresponding therapeutic interventions that will change behavior.
   b. as well as the concerns of the other paradigms.
   c. and attempts to explain the functioning of the unconscious.
   d. but tends to ignore pretty much everything else.

   Answer: d   Page: 508
   Topic: The Different Approaches

3. One view of the different personality approaches is that each
   a. is addressing the same basic questions as the other approaches.
   b. addresses fundamentally different questions.
   c. leaves something out.
   d. b and c.

   Answer: d   Page: 509
   Topic: Which One Is Right?

4. According to the text, you should judge a personality approach by which of the following criteria?
   a. Correctness
   b. Ability to explain unconscious processes

c. Usefulness
d. Ability to integrate affective and cognitive mechanisms

Answer: c   Page: 509
Topic: Which One Is Right?

5. One prediction about the future of the cognitive approach is that it will
   a. be rejected as unscientific.
   b. focus almost exclusively on determining memory capacity.
   c. examine how information processing affects interpersonal behavior.
   d. circumvent the need to include emotion variables' descriptions of personality systems.

Answer: c   Page: 515
Topic: Further Developments of the Cognitive Approach

6. The application of computer models to understanding the workings of the human mind has revealed ways in which people are *not* like computers. This realization has been called
   a. the computer error.
   b. the computational paradox.
   c. the bio-cognitive bias.
   d. none of the above.

Answer: b   Page: 515
Topic: Further Developments of the Cognitive Approach

7. The human mind is unlike a computer in that people
   a. are aware.
   b. experience emotions.
   c. process very little information.
   d. a and b.

Answer: d   Page: 515
Topic: Further Developments of the Cognitive Approach

8. In the future, one view is that biological approaches to personality will
   a. identify a specific brain structure that determines personality.
   b. recognize that personality is not linked to genetics.
   c. focus on how biological processes affect personality.
   d. become unnecessary for understanding personality.

Answer: c   Page: 418
Topic: Biology

204 | *Chapter 19*

9. It has been suggested that the future challenge of cross-cultural psychology will be
   a. to recognize that cross-cultural comparisons are just not possible.
   b. to identify constructs that are general enough to allow cross-cultural comparisons.
   c. to see each culture in its own terms.
   d. a and c.

   Answer: b   Page: 517
   Topic: Cross-cultural Psychology

10. Current research on the accuracy of personality judgments is an example of
    a. how personality, social, and cognitive psychology can be integrated.
    b. the future direction of biological approaches to personality.
    c. a research paradigm that will not exist in the future.
    d. an integration of psychoanalytic and behavioral approaches to personality.

    Answer: a   Pages: 517–518
    Topic: Integration of Personality, Social, and Cognitive Psychology

11. The only way to determine if your understanding of a person's personality is correct is
    a. to determine if it can account for everything about the person.
    b. to try to use it to explain or predict what the person does.
    c. to use it to uncover their unconscious motivations.
    d. none of the above.

    Answer: b   Page: 518
    Topic: The Quest for Understanding